Preventing and Managing Violence in Organizations

Preventing and Managing Violence in Organizations
Workplace Violence, Targeted Violence, and Active Shooters

Marc H. Siegel

CRC Press
Taylor & Francis Group
Boca Raton London New York

CRC Press is an imprint of the
Taylor & Francis Group, an **informa** business

CRC Press
Taylor & Francis Group
6000 Broken Sound Parkway NW, Suite 300
Boca Raton, FL 33487-2742

Library of Congress Cataloging-in-Publication Data

Names: Siegel, Marc H., author.
Title: Preventing and managing violence in organizations : workplace
violence, targeted violence, and active shooters / Marc H. Siegel.
Description: 1 Edition. | Boca Raton, FL : CRC Press, [2019] | Includes
bibliographical references and index.
Identifiers: LCCN 2018037945 | ISBN 9781138496811 (hardback: alk. paper)
Subjects: LCSH: Violence in the workplace. | Offenses against public
safety. | Risk management.
Classification: LCC HF5549.5.E43 S54 2019 | DDC 658.4/73—dc23
LC record available at https://lccn.loc.gov/2018037945

Visit the Taylor & Francis Web site at
http://www.taylorandfrancis.com

and the CRC Press Web site at
http://www.crcpress.com

I dedicate this book to my wife and best friend, Linda; my daughters Dahlia, Maya and Emma; my son-in-law, Preston; and last but certainly not least, my granddaughter, Marni. Marni was a great stimulus for writing. She helped me focus so I would have more time to spend with her.

I would also like to acknowledge the support of my family members in writing this book. Their patience in listening to me while I bounced ideas off them has been invaluable. I especially would like to thank Maya for helping with the editing and making suggestions for improvements.

CONTENTS

SECTION III   Tactics and Control Measures

SECTION IV   Closure

LIST OF FIGURES

AUTHOR

Dr. Marc H. Siegel is President and CEO of M Siegel Associates LLC and the Director of Global Security and Resilience Projects, Homeland Security Graduate Program at San Diego State University, USA. He served as the Commissioner heading the ASIS International Global Standards Initiative developing international and national risk management, resilience, security, and supply chain standards. He is an internationally recognized Certified Lead Auditor, Trainer and Skills Assessor for risk, resilience, and security management. At San Diego State University, he pioneered the concept of applying a systems approach to risk, resilience, and security management for organizations and their supply chains. He works with several multinational companies on supply chain risk management. He chaired the technical committees and working groups for 13 ANSI American National standards for risk, resilience, and supply chain management including the series developed for private security service providers to demonstrate accountability to business and risk management requirements while meeting legal obligations and respecting human rights. He served as Chairman of ISO/PC284 developing standards for private security service providers. He is coauthor *of Organizational Resilience: Managing Risks of Disruptive Events – A Practitioner's Guide*, by James Leflar and Marc Siegel, CRC Press, 2013.

Section I

Introduction

1

Introduction

FOCUS ON AWARENESS AND CULTURE

No one can assume that they are immune from violence. Violence may occur in any location or in any organization whether it be in a workplace, school, or house of worship. While the likelihood of a violent event occurring may be relatively small, the consequences of an event are often severe to the organization and people associated with it. Therefore, organizations have a duty of care to develop programs, policies, and procedures to minimize the likelihood and consequences of violent acts. "It can't happen here," and other forms of denial are simply bad management practice and negligence on the part of the organization. Workplace violence, active shooters/assailants, and targeted violence can occur in any type or size of organization. Therefore, it is necessary to plan how to prevent, prepare for, respond to, and recover from such events.

Note in this book the term "targeted violence" will be used to denote active shooter, active assailant, and terroristic attacks. All of these events share the trait of an insider or outsider committing a violent act against an individual or groups of people within or outside the organization's physical boundaries.

In today's world of 24/7 mass communications, there is a perception that targeted violence should constantly consume your life with fear. Giving in to this fear is in fact one of the motivating factors underlying terroristic acts. This book provides tools to better prevent, prepare for, and manage violence in an organization (and community). Proper planning to prevent and manage the risk of violence in organizations empowers people to go about their daily lives and business with skills needed to address issues if they should arise. Targeted violence is not always preventable, but awareness and preparedness can mitigate the hazards.

This book emphasizes the importance of building a security and risk culture in an organization that focuses on human behaviors and awareness. In every aspect of your life, you are a risk maker and a risk taker; therefore, you have a personal responsibility to be a risk manager. Your safety and resilience depend on how you manage the risks you confront. While law enforcement and security professionals play an important role in keeping our businesses, schools, and houses of worship safe, it is important to take responsibility for yourself and the people around you. Top management and persons at all levels of an organization have a role to play in promoting security and risk awareness throughout the organization.

This book primarily focuses on programs, policies, and procedures that can be implemented by managers and other laypersons. It is not written solely for law enforcement and security professionals. Building security and risk awareness starts with a realization that security and safety depend on you. It is not something you can ignore in the belief that law enforcement and security professionals will handle security for you. Think of security and risk management as a computer operating system. Designed appropriately, it is something that operates seamlessly in the background so that you can focus on what you want to accomplish.

Managing workplace violence and targeted violence is a complex issue because they are dependent on human behaviors. Assailants and other perpetrators of violence exhibit a wide range of behaviors that always seem clearer in hindsight. People from different religions, nationalities, cultures, economic classes, and educational backgrounds may exhibit different behaviors and have different beliefs and value systems, which are completely normal, but may not be what you are used to. This is a major challenge that needs to be recognized from the outset: that if someone is different, or even "odd," it does not mean they are automatically a threat or a person of concern. When developing behavioral indicators and program parameters, care must be taken to consider the diversity of the people the program will address. Focusing on someone simply because they have a different background may actually distract you from noticing someone exhibiting behavioral indicators.

PERSPECTIVE OF BOOK

This book views the prevention and management of violence in organizations as a risk and business management issue; therefore, the main objective of this book is to help organizations develop a program for preventing and managing violence that can be integrated into its day-to-day overall business management approach. For organizations that have adopted an ISO, Robust Process Improvement, or Six-Sigma management systems approach, they will immediately recognize that the elements described in the framework can be integrated seamlessly into their overall management system approach.

Did you ask a good question? Answers are important but asking a good question can provide better insight and understanding. Questions can lead to answers we never thought to ponder until we asked the question. The depth of understanding often comes from answering a question with a question.

Organizations exist to pursue their objectives and create value in the products and services they provide. Therefore, providing a safe and secure environment within the organization, and with regard to all the organization's activities, is a core management imperative. Many, if not most, organizations do not have a dedicated chief security officer to oversee the prevention and management of violence. Furthermore, many resource allocation decisions are made by business managers, not the security manager. Therefore, there is a need for risk and business managers to understand how security-related and other disruptive risks impact the achievement of the organization's objectives. This book focuses on program development and implementation from a business management perspective. It will help risk and business managers understand the concepts and ask educated questions about how to prevent and manage violence.

Security practitioners will also find this book useful in designing security programs that integrate security into the day-to-day activities of the organization. It will help them better explain how to integrate security into the organization's system of management and activities. It will help them present prevention and management of violence from a business management perspective to support the overall objectives of the organization. It demonstrates the value-added from investments in security.

Many of the concepts in this book can be explored to also enhance security and safety in our homes and communities. There is no one-size-fits-all approach, all the information in this book should be tailored to your organization's culture and management style, as well as to the risk environment. This book provides a recipe of ingredients for managing the risk of violence in an organization. It is written like a recipe book—it outlines the ingredients; then you must determine the amounts and order of blending the ingredients to fit your needs, tastes, and budget.

ORGANIZATION OF BOOK

This book focuses on establishing and implementing a system of management (aka framework or management system) for preventing and managing violence in organizations. The first part of this book provides a discussion of the importance of building a security and risk management culture in the organization. This is followed by an overview of the different types of violence and threat actors that an organization should consider. The planning process and getting started on establishing the program introduces the systems approach that will be used to establish the framework.

The second part of this book addresses how to build the framework. This section describes the elements that comprise a robust management system. The framework is consistent with management systems used in business and risk management. This will enable seamless integration of the framework into the overall system of management.

The third part of this book provides additional tactical information about how to conduct the activities described in the framework section. The focus is on how to formalize the prevention and management of violence using risk management tools common to a range of risks. Again, the message is preventing and managing violence is a day-to-day activity that needs to be incorporated into all the activities and functions of the organization.

The concluding section of this book provides some closing thoughts and a list of resources available from free public sources that readers can use to seek additional information.

2

Understanding Your Risk Environment

Risk factors vary significantly depending on the type, location, physical setting, and activities of an organization. They are also influenced by the political, social, and cultural environment of the organization. Behaviors that create anxiety, fear, and mistrust in the organization need to be considered when creating a program to manage the risk of violence in an organization. These behaviors can take the form of physical contact, direct or indirect threats (verbal or written), bullying, stalking, sexual harassment, intimidation, and/or cyber threats.

When defining the risk environment and the risks facing the organization, it is important to keep in mind that many people have a false impression of their

The United States Occupational Safety and Health Administration defines workplace violence as follows:
Workplace violence is any act or threat of physical violence, harassment, intimidation, or other threatening disruptive behavior that occurs at the work site. It ranges from threats and verbal abuse to physical assaults and even homicide. It can affect and involve employees, clients, customers and visitors.
www.osha.gov/SLTC/workplaceviolence/

risk environment. This may be due to the coverage of sensational events. Multiple homicide and terroristic events comprise a very small percentage of events of violence in organizations. It is more likely that the

7

organization will need to address "day-to-day" incidents that do not get media exposure such as threats, assaults, bullying, physical and/or emotional abuse, harassment (sexual, racial, and/or religious), stalking, and domestic violence. It is important to consider the sensational events, but over-focusing on these types of events diverts precious resources from addressing the day-to-day types of incidents that are more likely to affect people associated with your organization.

Violence is typically due to either predatory/planned or impulsive/reactive behaviors of a threat actor (sometimes called an "adversary," "person of concern," "hazardous agent," "assailant," or "perpetrator"). Regardless of what they are called, they are human beings—a varied and often unpredictable species. Impulsive/reactive behaviors are unplanned and emotional responses to a stimulus (e.g. a perceived threat). Predatory/planned behaviors are typical of targeted violence (e.g. terroristic and active shooter/assailant events), which are very seldom spontaneous events. They are premeditated and designed to fulfill the objectives of the threat actor. Targeted violence events (e.g. active shooter/assailant situations) are unpredictable and evolve quickly. This means a program to manage the risks of violence in an organization that considers monitoring behaviors and implementing proactive measures related to identified triggers may have a better chance of preventing or mitigating a violent event.

There are many things that will determine the types of violence that the organization may need to address, such as occupational group and industry sector, location of activities, and types of internal and external interactions. The United States Occupational Health and Safety Administration and the Federal Bureau of Investigation define four types of workplace violence based on the relationships between the threat actor and targets. Two additional types have been added here which are additional types of violence organizations may encounter. Examples of types of violence include the following:

- Type I: Violent acts perpetrated by external threat actors with criminal intent with no direct connection to the organization (e.g. robbery, theft, assault). Typically, these are irregular occurrences in normal operations of any particular at-risk organization. These types of events are the most common to result in fatal outcomes. Certain occupations (taxi drivers, night workers, convenience store employees, health-care workers, cash-and-carry operations) and/or persons in isolated or dangerous locations are more likely to encounter violence. Many of these acts are driven by a sense of social or political injustice where the manifestation of the violence is linked with local cultural norms. Mitigation techniques rely on situational awareness training, administrative policies, and physical security measures (guards, barriers, surveillance, access control, locks, lighting, weapon detectors, etc.).

- Type II: Violent acts can happen to persons working on behalf of the organization by an external threat actor to whom they are providing a service. These may be due to impulsive/reactive behaviors of a customer who feels aggrieved by service not meeting their expectations. In some occupations, the threat is inherent with the dealing with aggravated, unstable, or dangerous people and can occur on a daily basis in many service establishments (e.g. health care, rehab and social welfare programs, customer service, educational institutions). Training in de-escalation techniques can help mitigate these types of events. Physical security measures, such as layout and design of facilities, barriers, access controls, and alarms, can be used in conjunction with de-escalation and awareness training.
- Type III: Violent acts may be committed by someone currently or previously associated with the organization against coworkers, contractors, supervisors, or managers. An individual may be seeking retribution for what is perceived as unfair treatment by a coworker or manager, or the act may be linked to threat actor psychosocial factors. Threats and other types of harassment, as well as fistfights, are more common outcomes than fatal violence. Grievance and reporting mechanisms coupled with monitoring behaviors for warning signs are important components of prevention and management planning.
- Type IV: Violent acts may be committed in an organization by persons not employed by the organization but who have a personal relationship with persons at the organization. Domestic or intimate partner violence seldom remains only at home. When a person has a dispute with a person working on behalf of the organization, the attack may be focused on a particular individual or group. Alternatively, location and tactics may be planned, but the choice of victims is random with intent to maximize casualties. Domestic and intimate partner violence support programs as well as grievance and reporting mechanisms coupled with monitoring behaviors for warning signs are important components of prevention and management planning.

- Type V: Violent acts may be committed by a threat actor who is acting on their fundamental beliefs. The TA justifies violence based on an extreme belief system or sense of being wronged (e.g. active shooters/assailants, "lone-wolf" terror and hate crimes). The threat actor believes that righting an injustice and/or promoting their ideological, political, social, and/or religious views make violence warranted and necessary. Targets represent a conflict with the extremist's belief system and/or their sense of being wronged. In the threat actor's mind, there is little room for reasoning. Often, location and tactics are planned, but the choice of victims is random with intent to maximize casualties. These events are very rare, but due to their significant impacts and spectacular nature, they attract significant media attention as well as generate widespread fear and anxiety. Physical security measures coupled with monitoring behaviors for warning signs are important components of prevention and management planning.
- Type VI: Violent acts may be committed by multiple threat actors working as a tactical unit (coordinated terror and hate crimes). The well-trained and prepared extremists believe that violence effectively promotes their cause, ideological, political, and/or religious views, making it justifiable, necessary, and warranted. They perceive their target as part of a pseudo-military operation. Multiple methods to cause harm may be deployed at multiple locations and may include hostage taking. These events are very rare, but due to their significant impacts and spectacular nature, they attract the most media attention as well as generate widespread fear and anxiety. Physical security measures coupled with monitoring behaviors for warning signs are important components of prevention and management planning.

> Active shooter definition:
> An active shooter is one or more individuals actively engaged in a random or systematic act, or attempt, of mass murder. Their intent is to continuously harm others. The situations are unpredictable and evolve quickly. Also referred to as "active assailants," "active killers," or "violent intruder."

For all the types of violence, prevention programs should emphasize everyone's responsibilities in monitoring observable behaviors for warning signs of potential violence and situational awareness. Preplanning and coordination with law enforcement and first responders, complemented by training in survival skills during the incident, helps minimize potential damage. In all types of violence, public and private security and safety professionals have a role to play, but individuals need to take responsibility and be trained on how to report concerns and respond appropriately.

Any of these types of violence can affect any type of organization at varying degrees. Since the type of violence and motivating factors for the violence may only be known after the event, it is important to include procedures and training programs to address all these types of violence in the organization's system of management. Many of the survival techniques are similar regardless of the type of violence.

It is important to assess your specific organization's exposure to these risks and determine the local context of how these types of violence can manifest themselves. For example, is your organization

Terrorism definition:
The use or threat of violence and intimidation, especially against civilians, in the pursuit of political, social, religious, or ideological aims and change.

located where there is easy access to potentially lethal weapons, and what is the local cultural acceptance of resolving problems with force?

In examining the above types of violence, it is clear that the threat can be either from an insider or outsider. Organizations should plan and prepare for both insider and outsider threats. Denial and "it can't happen here" are not acceptable solutions. Any of the above types of violence can happen to any organization. Therefore, it is incumbent on all organizations to consider all these scenarios in their planning processes.

It is important to identify and assess factors that may increase the likelihood violence associated with the types of activities the organization engages in and the internal and external influences. There is no one-size-fits-all approach. The organization's activities and location, coupled with human factors, are considered in developing the tailored approach. Assessing the risks of violence in an organization requires assessing the internal and external factors that influence the risk, then developing plans tailored to the risk environment, culture, needs, resources, and objectives of the organization.

The goal of any risk management program is to protect human, tangible, and intangible assets. A violent act may irreparably damage an organization's reputation, brand, intellectual property, and mental well being of persons associated with the organization. Prevention will never achieve 100% results; therefore, response and continuity plans must consider the intangible assets of human well-being and reputation.

It is easy for us to become engrossed in worry about the last spectacular event. The system to prevent and manage violence in the organization should consider all types of violence. However, it is important not to lose site of the big picture. The majority of violence that affects the majority of organizations is related to day-to-day activities not the rare spectacular event. Plan for both, not just the spectacular.

3

Program Planning Process

Planning is critical for an effective system to prevent and manage violence in the organization. An organization should have a planning process that includes the following elements:

- Analysis of the internal and external factors that contribute to the risks related to violence
- Identification of human, tangible, and intangible assets that may be impacted by violence
- Identification of threat scenarios, hazards, and corresponding risks
- Identification of applicable legal, regulatory, contractual, and other requirements
- Setting of objectives and targets and establishment of procedures to achieve them
- Establishing performance criteria and conducting performance evaluations
- Addressing root causes of issues to drive continual improvement

A planning process encompassing the above components can help an organization focus its resources on those areas that are most important to the achievement of its goals. Information generated by the planning process can also be used in the establishment and improvement of other parts of the system of management, such as training, operational control, monitoring, and change management.

Planning is an ongoing process. It is used both to establish and implement elements of the system of management and to maintain and improve them based on changing circumstances as well as inputs and outputs of the system of management itself. The iterative planning process considers how to measure and evaluate the performance of the system of management in terms of meeting policy commitments, objectives and targets, and other performance criteria to identify opportunities for improvement. Therefore, it is useful to establish performance indicators during the planning process.

An effective system of management to prevent and manage violence in an organization should seamlessly integrate into the organization's overall system of management. Therefore, as with any management system, it should include the following elements:

> "Plans are worthless, but planning is everything. There is a very great distinction because when you are planning for an emergency you must start with this one thing: the very definition of 'emergency' is that it is unexpected, therefore it is not going to happen the way you are planning."
>
> Dwight D. Eisenhower,
> National Defense Executive Reserve Conference in Washington, D.C.
> (November 14, 1957)

- Articulating a policy statement/management commitment
- Understanding the needs and context of the organization
- Identifying and prioritizing significant risks, threats, vulnerabilities, and impacts
- Developing objectives with measurable targets
- Identifying and allocating authorities, resources, and competence requirements
- Designing and implementing of action plans to meet objectives and targets
- Developing targeted awareness and training programs
- Checking, testing, and following-up corrective and preventive actions
- Management review driving continual improvements

When establishing a program to prevent and manage violence, the following general principles should be considered:

1. Top management support and commitment is essential. Effective programs are built with committed leadership. In addition to establishing the policies and allocating resources, top management should lead by example.
2. People are your most important asset. Technology can help, but it is not a substitute for a risk and security awareness culture. It

is essential to designate threat assessment and incident management teams with defined structure, roles, and responsibilities.

3. Plans should be adaptive and proactive, not simply reactive. Programs should emphasize building resilience in the organization and the persons working on its behalf. Prevention and mitigation measures should be implemented to minimize both the likelihood and consequences of a violent event.

4. Violence in an organization is more than just physical assaults. Verbal abuse, intimate partner violence, threats, harassment, intimidation, bullying, emotional abuse, stalking, and other forms of behavior intended to create stress and anxiety should be considered.

5. The program is tailored to the organization and its risk environment. There is no one-size-fits-all approach. Plans, procedures, and drills should be tailored to the needs, resources, risk environment, and culture of a particular organization.

6. A system to manage the risk of violence in an organization should be integrated into the overall management system of the organization and its day-to-day activities. Awareness for preventing violence should be seamlessly integrated into all activities.

7. Understand the cultural, human, and managerial characteristics of the organization and people with whom it interacts. Management styles and work atmosphere should de-escalate levels of stress, frustration, and intimidation while projecting a sense of even-handedness and fairness.

8. Understand the tangible and intangible costs of violence to the organization, its people, and the community. Violence can damage the organization's image, trust, and sense of security and safety in addition to physical damage and lost productivity.

9. Planning for, preventing, and responding to violence requires an inclusive top-down, bottom-up approach that uses a multi-disciplinary team approach. Expertise should be sought from a number of perspectives.

10. Plan for post-incident support for the people affected by violence. Most people are affected by exposure to high stress and violence. Plan for recovery to a "new normal" after an incident.

11. Formal communications mechanisms are essential. Management should actively communicate policies. Mechanisms to communicate warning signs that are an indication of problems should be articulated and used. Prevention plans need to be effectively communicated to appropriate parties.

15

12. Communications should be timely. Time is an incredibly important factor in managing violence in an organization. Both incoming and outgoing communications need to be responsive and timely.
13. Training and awareness are key to success. Training and awareness programs must be tailored to the target audience to be successful. All persons working on behalf of the organization should be aware of risks that impact them and which they may impact.
14. Employee assistance programs (EAP), injury and illness prevention programs (IIP), and/or domestic violence programs (DVP) should be integrated into the system of management for violence.
15. Plans are ongoing and dynamic not simple static documents. Exercising and testing of plans with all persons working on behalf of the organization supports effective implementation in the event of an incident. Exercises should be designed to test the plans as well as identify opportunities for improvement. Management should lead by example and participate in exercises.
16. Documentation provides clarity and protection. Clearly written action plans both guide and document activities. Records should be timely and detailed enough to provide possible liability protection.
17. Continually reevaluate and improve the plans. Personnel, the risk environment, business, and society are dynamic and change. Plans should be reviewed and revised when changes occur in the risk environment, based on exercise results, after the occurrence of an incident or near miss, and at predetermined management intervals.

4

Getting Started
Initial Information Gathering—
Gap Analysis

Establishing a system of management to prevent and manage violence in an organization requires an implementation strategy to drive cultural change. A cultural change of risk and security awareness in the organization is built on a top-down, bottom-up approach. It recognizes that time and other resources are limited commodities so people need to see value in the changes proposed. This requires implementing your plan at a pace that will keep people interested and engaged. People need to understand how the new activities complement their normal day-to-day activities. Start with focusing resources on critical issues that generate a sense of making the work environment more safe and secure. Success breeds success, so a better sense of well-being will help stimulate a corresponding sense of ownership and inclusion.

To effectively begin the initial review, top management should issue an organization-wide announcement of intent, endorsement, and commitment. Management should articulate the rationale for a program, linking it to the overall objectives of the organizations (e.g. improved morale and productivity, better delivery of services, concern for persons working on behalf of the organization).

Linking the program objectives to the overall organizational objectives emphasizes that the program is seen as an integral part of the value generating activities of the organization and not simply an additional burden.

Selecting a program leader to champion and manage the program is an important choice. The person need not be a security expert but should have the necessary authority and management support, understand the organization and its workings, and have project management skills. A "systems thinker" who can understand how the pieces of the puzzle fit together is more effective than someone who uses a simple linear check-box approach.

The next step is to build an implementation team with representation from key management functions (e.g. human resources, legal, production and/or service, maintenance, finance, safety, security, quality, administration, engineering, finance, labor and worker representatives). Team efforts are more effective in identifying issues, risks, opportunities, and existing processes. Contractors, suppliers, commercial building owners for leased properties, and other external parties (e.g. law enforcement, emergency responders) should also be considered as they will be impacted and can impact your operations. A cross-functional team can provide a breadth of perspectives, suggest measures that are in sync with the organization's value creation activities, and build a sense of inclusion and ownership.

After the team has been selected, conduct an orientation meeting to discuss the organization's objectives and the objectives and scope of the system to prevent and manage violence. Also, discuss the estimates of the time and resources required to complete the initial review, and the time and resources required to complete the entire project. The project leader should be reconfirmed and management's commitment should be reiterated.

The team is now ready to conduct the initial review and gap analysis to assess the organization's current position and opportunities for improvement. The aim of this review should be to consider the threats, hazards, and corresponding risks of the organization's facilities, activities, products, and services as a basis for establishing the system of management. Organizations with an overall management system should

---

Systems approach and thinking: A system is any set of distinct elements that interact to form a complex whole. A systems approach stresses that in addition to understanding the distinct elements, it is essential to understand the interactive nature and interdependence of the elements within the context of the external and internal factors affecting an organization. Component elements are designed and fitted together to achieve overall objectives. Feedback loops are an integral part of a systems approach.

---

familiarize themselves with the system to better integrate the prevention and management of violence into their overall approach to management.

The review should cover the following key areas:

- Identification of people, assets, services, products, activities, and functions that could be impacted by violence
- Identification of threats, hazards, and corresponding risks, including those associated with normal operating conditions, unusual and after-hours conditions, start-up and shutdown, and emergency situations and accidents
- Identification of applicable legal requirements and other requirements (e.g. privacy rights, social media policies, information sharing, and contractual requirements)
- Examination of existing security, safety, and emergency management practices and procedures, including those associated with outsourcing, procurement, and contracting activities
- Evaluation of previous incidents, emergency situations, near misses, and accidents and the effectiveness of incident/emergency preparedness and response plans

Before discussing the questions below, it is prudent to review other emergency response, business continuity, and security management policies, plans, and procedures in the organization. Fire protection, security, and natural disaster plans also address facility evacuation, assembly areas, notification systems, drills and exercises, first aid, and recovery. Start by reviewing these programs and study what lessons can be learned. Many of the practices in these programs need to be considered when planning the prevention and management of violence in an organization. Determine what can be leveraged and what might lead to confusion or conflicts. Integrated programs addressing a range of risks are more efficient. Siloing of different types of risk into separate programs can lead to confusion in responses, especially in the "heat of the moment" when an incident is unfolding.

Examples of questions to discuss during the review include the following:

- Questions related to understanding the potential for violence:
  - Does the organization have a significant risk of a Type I, II, III, IV, V, and/or VI violence event?
  - What are the operations and activities conducted by the organization that would be considered to have higher risk of violence?

19

- What are the physical characteristics and the activities conducted by the organization that may affect the security and safety of people working on its behalf?
- Have incidents of Type I, II, III, IV, V, and/or VI violence occurred in the past? If so, how often and what was their severity? Are the existing control measures sufficient to prevent and/or mitigate the incidents?
- What measures were taken by the organization to analyze the causes of any potential or real incidents? What corrective measures were taken to prevent other incidents?
- If your property is leased, what are the safety and security responsibilities and arrangements with the commercial building owner? Are there other tenants that can impact your risk or that you may impact?
- Are there other businesses or residences adjacent to your organization that could impact your security or that you may impact?
- What is the street access to the organization? Is there ingress and egress for emergency responders?
- Are cash transactions conducted during normal or after working hours? Are cash or other valuables stored at the facility? If yes, how are valuables stored and transported?
- What is the nature and frequency of interactions with costumers, clients, patients, or other contacts? Could any of these be considered adversarial or high stress?
- Do persons working on behalf of the organization travel or work off-site (particularly in high-risk areas and in remote locations)?
- What are the applicable legal and other requirements, including liability issues, that need to be considered (e.g. privacy, antidiscrimination, duty of care)?
- Questions related to understanding the context and environment for risk:
  - What is the history of assaults or the exhibiting of belligerent, intimidating, or threatening behavior in the workplace by either people working on behalf of the organization or people they interface with?
  - What are the crime levels in the area(s) of operation? What is the nature of the crime (violent or nonviolent)?
  - Is crime due to individual actions, organized crime, hate crimes, or gang violence?

- What are the perceptions of the risk of violence in the organization and community?
- What is the local cultural attitude of using force to solve problems?
- What is the access to weapons and what types? Are weapons and ammunition readily available that could be used by a threat actor for a mass-victim attack?
- What is the attitude toward domestic or intimate partner violence in the organization and the community? Is it something that is hidden or shared with others?
- Is there a sense of animosity due to social, political, religious, or economic inequality and injustice in the general community?
- What are the attitudes toward gender-based violence, including reporting of incidents?
- How are minorities and people who exhibit different behaviors and customs perceived in the organization and in the community?
- How does the community perceive your organization and its activities?
- What are the rates and attitudes toward alcohol and drug use in your organization and the community?
- What is the perception of stability in employment status? What is the turnover rate?
- How are layoffs, reduction-in-force actions, and disciplinary actions such as suspensions and terminations handled?
- If someone feels aggrieved, are there outlets and mechanisms to vet the issues (e.g. grievance or whistleblower mechanisms, management contacts)?
- Is there access to employee assistance programs (EAP) and/or injury and illness prevention programs (IIP) that address violence at your organization?
- Questions related to understanding the current status of the system of management to prevent and manage violence:
  - How has top management demonstrated its commitment to preventing and managing violence?
  - Does the organization have a clearly articulated and communicated policy(s) to prevent and manage violence?
  - What are the current programs for preventing and managing violence in the organization and/or other emergency

21

management plans? Are they well communicated? Are they effective?

- How does the organization conduct threat assessments and intervention strategies?
- How does the organization foster a climate of trust and respect among persons working on its behalf?
- What are the mechanisms that exist to communicate concerns? How are reports of concerns handled?
- Who are the persons in the organization tasked with overseeing the system of prevention and management of violence? Do they operate as a team? Are there other persons who should be included?
- What is the involvement of law enforcement and first responders with the organization's programs?
- Have incidents occurred at the main facility, satellite locations, and/or to persons conducting job-related functions off-site?
- What is the organization's method of determining the tangible and intangible costs of violence?
- Has management been trained on communication protocols for persons to report concerns and/or managing issues related to persons of concern?
- Does the organization provide orientation and ongoing regular training in preventive, response, and recovery measures for all new or current personnel, supervisors, and managers? If yes, how is this conducted?
- Does the organization have a code of conduct and other policies establishing standards of professionalism?
- Is there a nondiscrimination, anti-harassment, non-retaliation, and/or privacy policy and has it been communicated?
- Does the organization have assistance programs supporting victims of workplace or intimate partner violence that encourage people to seek help (and avoid guilt and punishment)?
- Does the organization have a clearly defined and communicated weapons policy that is consistent with jurisdictional laws?
- What are the organization's background screening and vetting for new and current persons working on its behalf? Is it reviewed at regular intervals?
- Does the organization have clearly defined and communicated privacy policies?

- Does the organization have clearly defined, fair, and consistent disciplinary procedures to project a sense of the right to due process?
- Does the organization have clearly defined and communicated cyber security and social networking protocols?
- Does the organization have clearly defined and communicated alcohol and drug usage policy?
- Are emergency contact numbers and grievance procedures clearly posted?
- Are reporting mechanisms, including the follow-up mechanisms clearly communicated?
- What mechanisms does the organization have to seek advice and assistance from outside resources (e.g. threat assessment practitioners, psychologists, psychiatrists, security professionals, social service agencies, legal and privacy experts, first responders, and law enforcement)?
- Questions related to the current status of physical security and emergency management plans:
  - Are there clear lines of vision inside and outside the facility, or are there obstructions to clearly seeing what is going on both inside and surrounding the facility?
  - Is the inside and outside of the facility, as well as the parking area, as brightly lit as permitted by jurisdictional law?
  - Do internal and external points of entry (e.g. doors, windows) have appropriately used locks? Is there a key control system?
  - What are the access and identification control measures used by the organization? Are authorized personnel approved before entry? Can unauthorized personnel be denied entry?
  - Are access control systems capable of accounting for the whereabouts of people?
  - Does the organization use closed-circuit television or other surveillance equipment capable of real-time tracking? Can the equipment assist law enforcement in locating the victims and threat actors?
  - Does the organization deploy detection technologies (e.g. weapons detectors, intrusion monitors, acoustic sensors)?
  - Can security equipment and technology be used in a dual-use manner for regular day-to-day activities?

- Are there clearly defined training, testing, and maintenance procedures for security equipment and technologies? How is its effectiveness tested?
- What sign-in and escort protocols does the organization practice?
- How are contractors, clients, customers, patients, and other persons' presence controlled at the facility?
- Is there an internal emergency response communication system? Does it provide warnings and/or tracking of people? Have people been trained on its use?
- Are there emergency alarms and call buttons and protocols?
- Are there barriers, safe rooms, and other lockable rooms that are bulletproof?
- What training programs exist for managing indicators of violence and emergency response?
- How does the organization account for persons working on behalf of the organization before, during, and after an incident?
- How does the organization communicate with persons (internal and external) during and after an incident? Is there a media liaison?
- Have one or more evacuation routes and assembly areas been designated? Have they been communicated and practiced? What are the estimated evacuation times? Have provisions been made for people with special needs?
- Are any obstructions (including clutter) blocking a quick exit?
- Have floor plans been communicated to persons responsible for safety and security, emergency response, and law enforcement?
- Does the organization have a business continuity plan and defined line of succession of authority?
- Does the organization have safety, security, emergency management, and business continuity plans? Can these be used and/or improved to address prevention and management of violence? Are they integrated?
- Does the organization have post-incident and recovery plans to address business resumption and caring for persons working on its behalf and their families?

In addition to the team discussions, other methods that can be used to answer the above questions to assess existing violence prevention management practices and procedures may include the following:

- Interviews with persons previously or currently working on behalf of the organization
- Evaluation of internal and external communications that have taken place with internal and external parties, including complaints, matters related to applicable legal requirements, media coverage, or past security or related incidents and accidents
- Review of incident and investigative reports
- Review of industry sectors and professional association reports of similar organizations
- Examination of law enforcement, crime statistics, and notification systems
- Gathering information related to current management practices

The results of the review are used to assist the organization in setting the scope of its system of management. The review provides the basis for developing or enhancing policies, setting of its objectives and targets, and determining the effectiveness of its approach for being in compliance with applicable legal requirements and other requirements (including contractual).

The initial review or gap analysis is, in itself, a microcosm of a well-organized approach to the entire planning process. The status of framework specifications, processes, procedures, and other recommendations of this book should be reviewed in the gap analysis. This includes policies, legal requirements, training, objectives and targets, operational control systems, document control, auditing, management review, and corrective action.

The review should consider the culture, products and services, marketing strategies, intangible assets (e.g. image and reputation), and other specifics of the organization. In all cases, consideration should be given to the full range of operating conditions, including off-hours, as well as possible incidents and emergency situations that may be encountered. The impact on the risk profile due to suppliers, outsource partners, subcontractors, and other persons working on behalf of the organization should be considered.

The review can be conducted using checklists, process flowcharts, interviews, direct inspection, and document examination. The results of the review should be documented so that it can be used to contribute to setting the scope and in establishing or enhancing the organization's system of management to prevent and manage violence.

Consultants may help in conducting the initial review and gap analysis, but they cannot do the work for the organization in isolation. Building a culture of security and risk awareness requires people within your organization being actively engaged throughout the development and implementation process. Some things to consider before using a consultant include the following:

- Assess the organization's in-house resources first.
- Examine available resources from professional societies and government agencies.
- Look for a consultant that is familiar with the local context and risk environment.
- Look for a consultant that is familiar with the organization's specific industry, services, and activities.
- Avoid consultants that express a prejudice or bias against specific groups of people.
- Given you are monitoring and managing human behavior, a threat assessment professional or forensic psychologist may provide different insights than a physical security practitioner, ex-law enforcement, or ex-soldier.
- Use consultants to gain insights on approaches used by other similar organizations.
- Make sure the organization and consultant are clear and in agreement about the scope and objectives of the work.

Based on the input from the initial review (gap analysis), the team should also address the following questions for planning the program for preventing and managing violence in the organization:

- Are there "low-hanging fruit" that can result in a quick success for the program which will heighten awareness and build confidence in the program?
- Was the implementation team leader effective in conducting the gap analysis? Is the implementation team the appropriate mix of people that will be needed for the threat management team and incident response team going forward, if not, how can the team be strengthened?

Section II

Building the Framework

5

Building the Framework— Key Elements

There is no need to reinvent the wheel. A system of management for preventing and managing violence in the organization will be much more effective if it seamlessly integrates with the organization's overall system of management. Therefore, start by asking what management model your organization uses. This book will use a very generic total quality management approach outlined in a plan-do-check-act (PDCA) or assess-protect-confirm-improve (APCI) model. These models are illustrated in the continual improvement diagram given in Figure 5.1. Figure 5.2 illustrates how key elements of the PDCA/APCI model are applied to building the framework for the system of management to prevent and manage violence in the organization.

The "framework" establishes a formal structure for the program to prevent and manage violence in the organization. Building the framework to correspond with the organization's

Do I need a framework?

The framework provides the management structure to turn policies, plans, procedures, and work instructions into actions. To be effective, a program needs to be "living" and dynamic. Without a framework, too frequently policies, procedures, and work instructions are just a discrete paper exercise. The key to a successful framework is to recognize that an integrated approach seamlessly blends managing risk with all the organization's core functions and activities.

29

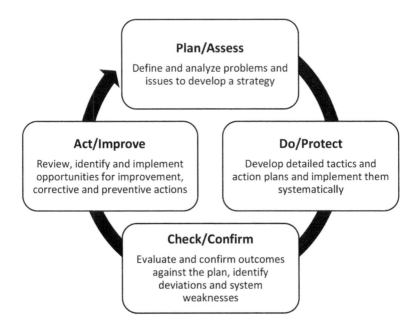

Figure 5.1 Plan-do-check-act or assess-protect-confirm-improve model.

system of management sends the message that security and risk aware-ness are a part of all day-to-day functions and activities. It is everyone's responsibility. Different sizes and types of organizations have different systems of management, both formal and informal. As with most orga-nizational programs, there is a need to have a framework that provides the skeleton to hold together the array of policies, plans, procedures, and work instructions. This book will first outline a framework describing the management elements needed to support the program. The subse-quent section of this book will provide details of how to develop the policies, plans, procedures, and work instructions that put the meat on the bones. When designing and building the framework, it is impor-tant to tailor the advice given in this book to the management context, culture, capabilities, and resources of the organization. The subtext for everything you design and implement should be addressing the follow-ing simple questions:

- Why am I doing this?
- Does this make people safer and more secure?

- Is this appropriate for the target audience?
- Do we have the adequate resources and commitment to achieve the program objectives?

Establishing a formal program to prevent and manage violence in the organization demonstrates that top management is addressing its duty of care to provide people who work on its behalf a safe and secure environment. The framework gives the organization the agility to adapt to a changing risk environment and tailor the program to its needs, obligations, and resources.

Common to most systems of management (aka management system) are the following key elements:

- Policy and management commitment—the policy is used to articulate management commitment and provide a foundation for planning and action. It sets the tone for establishing plans and procedures. It is the organization's commitment to manage the risks of violence in the organization.
- Risk and threat assessment—an analysis of the risk environment and the internal and external factors that may influence the achievement of objectives. It includes assessing the likelihood and impact of threats, vulnerabilities, and consequences.
- Legal and other requirements—identifying relevant laws, regulations, and liability issues, as well as other requirements (e.g. contract requirements, human rights codes) and assessing how they impact the organization.
- Setting objectives and targets —establishing goals for the organization, based on the policy and risk assessment, considering the interests of affected parties.
- Strategic programs—planning actions to achieve the objectives and targets considering resources needed.
- Structure and responsibility—assigning roles, responsibilities, and authorities for implementation of risk and other operational controls. Identify and allocate appropriate resources to support the program.
- Training, awareness, and competence—ensuring people working on behalf of the organization are trained and competent to carry out their responsibilities.
- Communication—establishing internal and external communication protocols and mechanisms.

- Documentation and document controls—maintaining information and records to support the program and procedures. Assuring the integrity and security of the information.
- Risk and other operational controls—identifying, planning, and managing the organization's activities and functions consistent with the policy, risk assessment, objectives, and targets.
- Incident management—risk management controls to address prevention, response, and recovery from potential undesirable and disruptive events.

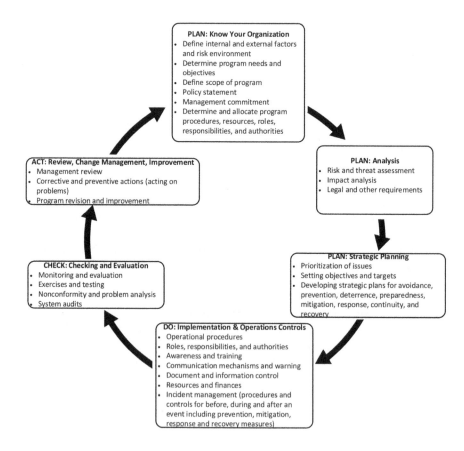

Figure 5.2 Components of system of management.

- Monitoring and measurement—ongoing monitoring of activities and tracking performance.
- Exercises—testing of procedures for efficacy, awareness, and to identify opportunities for improvement.
- Audit—verification of the system of management and its components.
- Management review—periodic review of the system of management to identify changing conditions and opportunities for improvement.

6

Building the Framework—Plan/Assess

Top management (senior leadership) has an obligation to provide a safe and secure environment in the organization. This is not just a moral obligation; it is also a legal or regulatory obligation in many legal systems and jurisdictions. In some jurisdictions, top management may be held personally liable for not providing adequate safety and security to persons working on their behalf. In addition, an organization's brand and reputation can be permanently damaged by violence in the organization, especially if it is perceived to have been avoidable. Building the framework provides the cohesion between policies, plans, and procedures. It provides documented evidence that the organization made a good-faith effort to carry out its duty of care.

Establishing the framework is similar to solving a complex mathematical problem. First, you must define the problem you are trying to solve. What are the parameters and variables that need to be considered? What are the simplifying assumptions and biases you bring to the solution? What are the boundary conditions that frame the problem? And how

> **Hindsight is 20/20**
>
> It is always easier to reevaluate plans, actions, or decisions after an event has happened. "It should have been obvious all along" follows many acts of targeted violence. Therefore, your framework, plans, and procedures must be regularly tested and exercised. Exercises and testing builds awareness, more efficient responses, and identifies opportunities for improvement.

do you document the process so that others can understand it? How do you check your work and determine if the solution indeed addresses the problem? Preventing and managing violence in the organization is a multidimensional, time-dependent problem. There is no one solution but multiple possibilities depending on how the problem solver perceives the problem.

A primary outcome of establishing the system of management framework is to build resilience in the organization, individuals, and the community. Resilience is the adaptability and agility of a community, organization, or individual to avoid, prevent, respond to, and recover from adversity. The system of management should consider what measures will help increase resilience and decrease uncertainty. It is seldom possible to eliminate all risks of violence, but it is possible to proactively prepare for violent events to better protect human, tangible, and intangible assets.

UNDERSTANDING THE ORGANIZATION AND ITS OBJECTIVES

The primary objective of any organization is to create value in the form of products and services. Businesses produce and market products and services. Educational organizations increase the knowledge base through research and teaching. Houses of worship create value by providing for people's spiritual needs and welfare. The program to prevent and manage violence in the organization needs to support these functions. Therefore, understanding the organization's mission, objectives, stakeholders, and the nature of its activities is essential. To understand the organization, start by asking the following questions:

1. What are the organization's core mission and short-, medium-, and long-term objectives?
2. What are the activities the organization engages in? What are the locations of these activities?
3. Who are the internal and external people who can impact risk and can be impacted by risk?
4. What is the makeup of the labor force? Are there particular areas of stress?
5. What is the interface with the public (community, clients, costumers, clientele)? Are there particular areas of stress or elevated risks of violence?

36

6. What are the social, political, economic, and demographic features of the local community that might make the organization more or less susceptible to violence?
7. What might motivate an adversary to conduct an act of violence against the organization and people working on its behalf?
8. What are the risks associated with the industry sector and the organization's activities and functions?
9. How might each of the previously discussed types of violence impact the organization and its human, tangible, and intangible assets?
10. What is the organization trying to achieve with its program to prevent and manage violence?

DEFINING THE OBJECTIVES OF THE PROGRAM TO PREVENT AND MANAGE VIOLENCE

As with any program, it is important to define the objectives. Program objectives should be aligned with the overall organizational and management objectives. "Eliminating all risks" is not an objective since it is not possible to eliminate all risks. Risk and uncertainty will always exist. Objectives should realistically examine what an organization has the capabilities, competence, and resources to improve. Given that most organizations have resource limitations, set your objectives to focus on major areas of concern and then use the framework to drive a continual improvement cycle to expand the organization's ability to cover a broader range of risks. Set the program objectives so that people working on behalf of the organization can sense an improvement in their well-being. Correct pacing of program rollout helps build cultural awareness. Trying to fix everything at once often leads to confusion and frustration as people become overwhelmed.

In setting program objectives, prioritize day-to-day risks and risks with the biggest impacts. A spectacular attack given extensive media coverage in another part of the world does not mean "you're next," especially if it is not necessarily consistent with your local risk environment. Keep in mind that there are endless scenarios for threats of violence, which will be determined by the adversary's capabilities (resources and knowledge) and motivation (intent, attractiveness, and confidence). When you examine your adversaries, determine how they might interact with your activities and functions.

Objectives should be reviewed by top management and preferably representatives from legal counsel. Top management will need to promote the objectives of the program in the policy statement and commitment of resources, while the legal team can advise the organization on potential legal and liability issues.

DEFINING THE SCOPE OF THE PROGRAM TO PREVENT AND MANAGE VIOLENCE

In conjunction with management, the organization should define and document a scope for the system of management. The scope should be based on the objectives of the program and take into consideration the organization's activities, internal and external obligations, and relevant legal and liability issues.

Scope may be enterprise-wide or limited to certain organizational units, activities, and/or locations. In keeping with the old saying: "Don't try to eat the whole the elephant in one bite," when getting started, define a manageable scope, consistent with resources, time, and levels of competence. The framework can be used as a pilot study to get the bugs out before expanding enterprise-wide.

Focus on the fact that you are trying to drive a risk and security awareness cultural change in the organization. Therefore, it must be paced with the capacity of the people in your organization to absorb changes. Over-scoping may result in insufficient focus to drive change, while under-scoping may result in key objectives being overlooked.

DEFINING AND DOCUMENTING ASSUMPTIONS AND BIASES

Assumptions are inherent to solving complex problems; therefore, they should be clearly defined and documented. Would other people make the same assumptions? What were the assumptions based on? Would the assessment have had different outcomes if the assumptions were different? Do the assumptions reflect a bias? By documenting your assumptions, it is possible for you and others to better evaluate the program outcomes and identify opportunities for improvement. Assumptions should be monitored and revisited as needed during the program life cycle.

38

All individuals have their own perspective on life. No two people's thought processes are exactly the same. Therefore, there is inherent bias in everything we do. Many people view groups that they do not belong to differently from people in groups they do belong to. It is important to understand how biases impact your perspective. Do we view things differently that we are familiar with? Do we show less empathy for peoples and cultures we are not familiar with? What is our concept of time? Are views being swayed by media exposure or crime statistics? Are we assuming people share our value system? Is our analysis based on representative data or simply the most available data? Understanding bias will help tailor the program to specific groups of people and locations.

MANAGEMENT COMMITMENT

For most programs in an organization to succeed, there is a need for active leadership and commitment from top management. This means walking the walk, as well as talking the talk. Management should oversee the establishment and implementation of the program as well as lead by example and motivate others to follow their lead. Direct, active participation of top management to support the programs includes the following:

- Establishing and communicating policies and objectives
- Providing adequate resources to support the program
- Assuring that competence needs are met with adequate training
- Setting up and serving on program oversight committee
- Visibly participating in drills and exercises with other members of the organization
- Making prevention of violence a topic of awareness and discussion in business and risk management meetings
- Monitoring program implementation and making sure issues raised are addressed in a timely fashion
- Participating in performance review process and evaluating and revising the policy as needed

Top management should clearly communicate to all levels of the organization the importance of the system of management to prevent and manage violence. Clearly linking the objectives of the program to the overall objectives of the organization and its day-to-day activities sends the message that the program is part of the overall governance priorities of the organization. Integrating support for the violence prevention and management procedures into individual performance reviews and recognition and rewards mechanisms helps promote the culture of risk and security awareness.

POLICY STATEMENT

A policy statement from top management serves as the foundational basis for the organization to set its objectives and targets. It reflects a commitment to prevent violence (when possible) and maintain a safe and secure environment in the organization. It establishes a code of conduct for people in the organization. It should cover activities both on-site and off-site that are related to the organization's activities.

The policy should be communicated to all persons working on behalf of the organization (internal and external personnel). The policy should be reviewed by people working on behalf of the organization when they start their affiliation with the organization, with refreshers at regular intervals.

The policy statement should make reference to the following:

> **Caution using zero-tolerance policies**
> A zero-tolerance policy assigns explicit, predetermined punishments to specific violations of organizational rules, regardless of the situation or context of the behavior. Sometimes, zero-tolerance policies can be counterproductive, limiting possible responses and communications needed to manage violence. Some zero-tolerance policies punish the victim who responds along with the guilty. There is not a presumption of innocence, and it treats all transgressions and individuals equally, regardless of age, intent, past behavior, or magnitude of the offense. Automatic suspension and expulsion may discourage people from speaking up. Also consider nonpunitive and evidence-based policies that take a more preventive approach that may have better results given the circumstances.

- Define the objective of the program—preventing violence and providing a safe environment free from harassment, intimidation, coercion, threats of violence, and any other behaviors that may cause intentional harm to others.
- Scope of policy—what and who is covered by the policy (e.g. full-time, part-time, contractual employees, and people who interface with the organization). Emphasize preventing violence in the organization is everyone's responsibility.

- Code of conduct—clearly define unacceptable behavior including the prohibition of direct or indirect threats of violence or behaviors that can cause others harm; prohibition of using organizational materials to threaten, intimidate, or harass others; prohibition of weapons at the organization; and commitment to respect legal and other requirements. Reinforce that communications are bidirectional and persons working on behalf of the organization have an obligation to report and inform appropriate persons about a potential for violent acts. Require good-faith reporting of suspicious behaviors and violations of the policy. Require active participation in risk and security awareness training and drills of the organization.
- Commitment statement—provide an open-door policy for reporting threats and incidents of violence with a commitment to thoroughly investigate the concerns in a timely fashion. Reference conflict resolution mechanisms, domestic or intimate partner violence and other employee assistance programs, and community resources. Encourage persons to bring issues to designated persons in the organization.
- Process statement—provide awareness of the reporting and complaints systems including a non-retaliatory statement for the good-faith reporting. Statement of commitment to conduct fact-based investigations in a fair and timely fashion respecting the dignity and privacy of concerned persons and persons of concern. Commit to maintain the integrity of investigations and their reporting. Outline the potential consequences for deviations from the policy and code of conduct.

Some organizations might have stand-alone policies for harassment and discrimination, weapons possession, code of ethics, social networking usage, communications, control substance use, and individual rights. The policy statement for preventing and managing the risk of violence should be reviewed for consistency with other related policies. Consolidate policies when possible to simplify training and retention of the policy content.

ESTABLISHING THE THREAT ASSESSMENT TEAM

To be effective, the program requires a dedicated team to assess the needs, risks, and threats of violence in the organization. The "threat management team" can have various names (threat assessment, risk assessment,

41

crisis assessment, etc.). Regardless of the name, the team needs the appropriate mix of individuals and competence to analyze risks, address reports of concerns, and implement control measures. They need the appropriate authority, communication skills, resources, and neutrality to credibly conduct their task. The threat management team may also serve as the incident management team. However, keep in mind that the same people who are good at analysis are not always equally as good at responding under stress. There should be a designated team leader who is familiar with the policy, program, and procedures; has an open door to top management; and who is viewed as fair and unbiased by persons working on behalf of the organization.

Teams typically work on a consensus basis. It is a decision-making process that seeks the input and perspective of all team members to reach a general agreement among the team members. Deviations from the generally accepted opinion or decision should be noted to document the vetting of issues and for review purposes.

The team should identify members from different divisions, functions, and activities in the organization. An interdisciplinary team can view information from different perspectives to review issues before forming a consensus. The size and complexity of the organization will determine the size of the team. Consider participants from human resources, process control, customer service, divisional management, legal, safety and health, and security managers, as well as representatives from unions and other labor representatives. Depending on the type of organization and its activities, it may be prudent to include commercial building owners for leased properties, members of industry associations, law enforcement, and first responders. As with any team effort, the roles, responsibilities, and authorities of the team members should be defined.

The team leader should review the competences needed to conduct an assessment of the needs, risks, and threats of violence. Training should be provided to the team to assure they are competent to conduct their assigned tasks. Training should emphasize the psychological and behavioral aspects of various forms of violence affecting the organization, how terminology and scales of measurement will be used in analyses, as well as the control measures used by the organization. The team leader should monitor team members for signs of stress, projecting biases, professionalism, and discretion.

Organizations may choose to seek external expertise to supplement the skills and knowledge of the team. It may be helpful to have the team trained by people with expertise in conducting risk assessments, security measures, and legal issues if these competences are not available in-house. Since the expression of threats may vary with cultures, it is important to seek external assistance from an expert who is not just a generic threat assessment expert but someone who is also familiar with the local culture and context. Unnecessary measures may be considered if threat experts base their analysis on "worst-case" scenarios that are not anchored in the culture, context, and risk environment of the organization.

LEGAL AND OTHER REQUIREMENTS

Laws, regulations, liability, and other obligations vary from jurisdiction to jurisdiction; therefore, it is necessary to evaluate the organization's obligations within the context of the jurisdictions that impact operations. The team, preferably with the input from legal counsel, should

- Identify laws, regulations, contractual, and other obligations (e.g. labor agreements, industry guidelines, human rights guidance) that are applicable
- Determine who is impacted and how they might impact compliance
- Determine how laws, regulations, liability, and other obligations affect activities and procedures
- Train people on the obligations associated with their activities and their role in compliance
- Inform and train relevant people on their rights and obligations
- Monitor any changes and compliance with laws, regulations, liability, and other obligations

When designing the monitoring, reporting, and risk control measures, it is necessary to understand and consider the privacy and confidentiality laws that are relevant to the jurisdictions of operations, as well as identify organizational policies. Laws and regulations can vary significantly in different jurisdictions. Monitoring, recording, and sharing access to communications and information may not be the same in all jurisdictions of operations, so legal counsel should be consulted when planning communication and information management procedures. Particular attention should be paid to moving and storing data and information across jurisdictional boundaries.

Liability protection and data retention requirements should be incorporated into program planning processes. Legal counsel should be

43

consulted to confirm that procedures are consistent with legal and contractual obligations as well as organizational policies. What documentation and recordkeeping procedures can help reduce liability concerns? Protecting the integrity of documents and records should consider data access, version control, retention, information security, archiving, obsolescence, and destruction.

CONDUCTING AN ASSESSMENT OF THE NEEDS, RISKS, AND THREATS RELATED TO VIOLENCE

A risk assessment provides insight into what can happen, how, when, where, why, and by whom. The risk assessment analyzing the risks due to violence in the organization can be conducted as a stand-alone assessment, but conducting the assessment as part of the overall risk assessment, or as part of the business continuity or security management programs, may lead to a clearer understanding how violence impacts other programs and activities. Also, consider the uncertainties in achieving the objectives of the system of management and program to prevent and manage violence.

Risk and threat assessments

Risk is the uncertainty in achieving strategic, tactical, operational, and reputation objectives. Simply put, a risk is the chance of something happening combined with consequences if it happened. Risk can have either negative or positive outcomes, but colloquially, the term is commonly used to imply negative outcomes. Focusing the assessment of risk on the uncertainty of achieving objectives rather than just bad events helps identify opportunities for improvement and key process indicators. Threats are sources of risk that result in undesirable or negative outcomes; therefore, threats are negative scenarios to be avoided or minimized. Certain threats may not be under the organization's control. Vulnerabilities are flaws or weaknesses in the system that can be exploited by threats to result in negative consequences. Vulnerabilities can be manipulated and minimized to decrease the likelihood and/or consequences contributing to the level of risk.

As used in this book, "risk assessment" will refer to activities related to program planning and implementation. "Threat assessment" will refer to assessing threat levels during program implementation (e.g. assessing the threat of a specific threat actor or person of concern).

The risk and threat assessments should be conducted by the multidisciplinary threat management team. The risk scenarios should be discussed by the group to collaboratively determine what risks are the most relevant and describe the characteristics and nature of the risk. Consider the following:

- How does the local context affect how a threat may manifest itself?
- How is the organization vulnerable to each of the threat scenarios?
- What would be the impact of the threat scenario materializing?
- What is the likelihood of an event?
- What are the consequences of an event and what is the likelihood these consequences will emerge during the event?
- What control measures are in place to prevent a violent act and monitor behaviors that are indicators of violence?
- What control measures are in place to mitigate the likelihood and consequences of the potential act of violence?
- What control measures are in place to address the response and recovery to an act of violence? How do these mitigate potential consequences?
- What control measures are dependent on law enforcement and first responders? What are their response times, capabilities, and coordination measures?
- How will an act of violence impact the brand, reputation, liability, morale of impacted persons, and the ability of the organization to continue to conduct its activities?
- How does the risk affect the achievement of the organization's objectives?

Many models exist for conducting risk assessments. The model chosen should reflect the overall risk assessment approach of the organization, the reliability and detail of the input information, and the makeup of the threat assessment team. A simplified model is depicted in Figure 6.1. It depicts an approach to identify, analyze, and evaluate risk in order to determine the appropriate risk control measures.

The risk assessment first identifies the assets, activities, objectives, and stakeholders (internal and external) who may impact or be impacted by violence in the organization. Consider the criticality of the assets assuming that the protection of life safety and the well-being of humans is the primary asset and objective. Image, brand, and reputation should also be considered a high criticality concern.

45

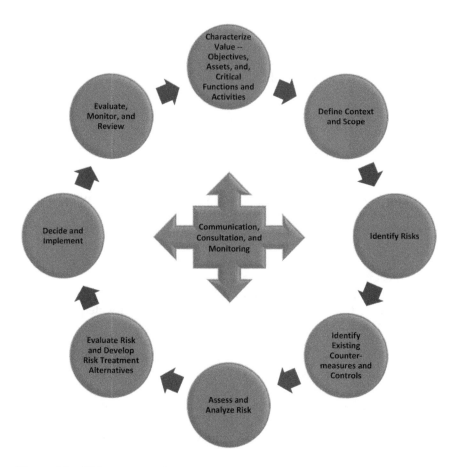

Figure 6.1 Risk assessment process.

Discuss potential scenarios that could result in violence, thereby hampering the organization's achievement of its objectives. Also, consider scenarios that would make it easier for the organization to achieve its objectives. There are endless scenarios; therefore, it is important to consider the scenarios within the context of the local physical, behavioral, and demographic realities. The intent and capabilities of threat actors as well as root causes of violence may vary significantly from one geographic location to another, so it is important to document your assumptions, biases, and definition of local context. For example, certain threat scenarios may be "typical" in high-crime areas where distinct root causes, cultural norms of tolerance, societal perspectives and support, and access to certain types of weapons exist. However, this does not mean in a low-crime area with a very different risk profile, similar threats will not play out in a similar manner. You cannot assume "it can't happen here," but the likelihood and consequences of certain scenarios for the different types of violence will change based on local conditions.

The discussion of potential scenarios should highlight what are the threats of violence the organization is facing. Keep in mind that assaults, intimidation, harassment, theft, domestic or intimate partner violence, childcare disputes, and service-related altercations are much more common than very rare yet spectacular events such as active shooters and terrorism. The risk assessment should consider all types of violence. Obviously, high likelihood–high-consequence events will be high-risk events and should be given top priority for treatment considering prevention, response, and recovery. Low likelihood–low-consequence events have a lower level of risk and are a lower priority for treatment. High likelihood–low-consequence events should be managed emphasizing prevention when possible. Low likelihood–high-consequence events need robust plans for before, during, and after an event. The low-likelihood but high-impact scenarios (active shooters, terrorism) generate the most fear and media attention as well as can result in irreparable consequences (physical, psychological, and reputational). Prevention, response, continuity, and recovery planning is needed for these types of events.

All steps in the risk assessment should be well documented. It is usually beneficial to maintain a risk register or catalog of the priority risks. Documentation of the risk assessment (including assumptions and biases) facilitates review of the process to measure changes and efficacy of programs, as well as identify opportunities for improvement.

SETTING PROGRAM OBJECTIVES, TARGETS, AND STRATEGIC PLANS

Objectives and targets are established to meet the goals articulated the organization's policy statement and commitment for the ongoing improvement of safety and security. Objectives and targets are developed from the results of risks assessments, legal and liability requirements, operational needs, and organizational priorities. The objectives and targets reflect the priorities given to managing the risks identified in the risk assessment. Setting the strategic objectives for managing risks will provide the necessary input into what tactics, procedures, and work instructions are needed to realize these objectives.

Objectives are strategic considerations such as better training programs, improved proactive communications, and/or better management of workplace violence. Targets are specific items (linked to performance indicators) such as refresher security awareness training of all employees within a one-year period, reduction of workplace violence by X% over a specified period of time, or an X% increase in productivity due to increased employee morale over the next year.

Since all organizations operate with some resource constraints, when setting objectives and targets, the organization should consider its financial, operational, and business limitations. Determine what objectives and targets are appropriate for your organization. Depending where the actions are needed, objectives and targets can be applied organization-wide or to individual units, divisions, or activities.

There are no specific numbers of objectives and targets that are appropriate for all organizations. An argument can be made that to drive a cultural shift, it is better to start with a limited, manageable number of objectives and expand the list with time. By keeping the list simple initially and addressing priority low-hanging fruit, it is more likely to achieve early success with the program and thereby generate excitement and interest. This helps promote a sense of inclusion, ownership, and well-being so critical to a cultural change.

A key objective of any program to manage violence in an organization is to raise security and risk awareness to promote a proactive culture in the organization. To achieve this, there is a need for both top management and persons responsible for achieving this objective to provide input into the development of the objectives, targets, and procedures to accomplish the desired change.

Strategic plans provide a roadmap for how the organization is going to turn its policy commitments, objectives, and targets into concrete actions. Leverage existing action plans for legal compliance, quality, continuity, security, health, and safety management. The strategic plans should consider administrative, methodological, technological, and engineering options for minimizing the risks before, during, and after an incident. Order of preference should be adaptive, proactive, and reactive approaches to emphasize prevention and protection. The mix of approaches will depend on operating parameters, goals, and persons involved.

Action plans should, at a minimum, describe the following:

- What issues are being addressed? Objectives and targets to achieve.
- Who will do it? Persons and responsibilities for achieving goals.
- How will they do it? Approaches and resources for achieving the goals.
- When? Time frames for achieving the goals.
- How will success be measured? Performance indicators for achieving goals.

The output of the risk assessment, objectives, targets, and strategic plans should be reviewed and approved by top management. The threat management team should clearly explain to top management the estimated residual risk (the risk and/or threat levels that remain after treatment) and any legal and liability concerns. It is not possible to eliminate all risks; therefore, top management needs to determine if the residual risk levels are within their level of acceptance or tolerance. Once there is agreement on the objectives, targets, and strategic plans, it is possible to begin development of tactics, procedures, and work instructions needed to realize these objectives.

7

Building the Framework—Implementation and Operational Controls

After top management and the threat assessment team agree on a strategic plan, it is time to develop the tactical approach of defining the program's procedures and work instructions. To be effective, the elements should be aligned and integrated with the organization's overall system of management. Not only does this reinforce the idea that security and risk awareness is always running in the background of all organizational activities, it also avoids conflicts with the organization's primary objectives and priorities. Children go to school to learn; the security and risk management procedures should facilitate this primary objective.

Human body analogy

The elements of a systems approach to management do not exist in isolation. They interact with each other, each playing an important function. If you want to understand how the human body works, you need to understand the workings of the heart, lungs, brain, etc., as well as how these parts interact with each other. When each is functioning properly and interacting together smoothly, you have a healthy body. It is a similar dynamic with a systems approach to management. It is a multifaceted, dynamic, iterative process, and not a linear process.

The elements of the framework described in this section are relevant to any system of management. They are similar to the elements one would consider for quality, environment, or business continuity management. So, review these programs. The framework elements might already exist and can be built on.

The elements described in this section turn the policy, objectives, and targets into action plans. Procedures and work instructions should be developed based on the identified risks for violence analyzed in the risk assessment. Well-defined operational procedures and work instructions are key risk management controls, so they should be aligned with the processes and activities they are trying to protect.

RESOURCES, ROLES, RESPONSIBILITY, AND AUTHORITY

For any system of management to be effective, roles, responsibilities, and authorities must be clearly defined and communicated. The commitment of all employees is needed for a system of management to live up to its full potential.

The size, availability of resources, and activities of an organization will dictate the roles and responsibilities in a system of management. Examine the core functions and activities of the organization and then determine how best to adjust the organizational structure to incorporate the program to prevent and manage violence. Also, keep in mind that external stakeholders such as contractors, outsource partners, supply chain partners, and temporary workers need to be considered. Flow-charting of existing processes, activities, and authorities is a starting point for understanding the organization's structure and how it can be leveraged to improve safety and security.

The top management should assign a program leader with sufficient authority, awareness, competence, and resources to ensure the establishment, implementation, and maintenance of the program. The individual should report to top management about performance and opportunities for improvement. Ideally, the program leader serves as champion of the program throughout the organization as well as has the ear of top management. The program leader should assemble teams with representation from all applicable levels of the organization. The program leader either serves as team leader or designates a leader for each team with specific tasking.

Depending on the organization's needs and overall organizational structure, the following team functions should be designated, either as discrete or combined teams:

- Threat management team—tasked with assessing risks to develop the program, analyze threats and persons of concern who are identified, and lead any preventive actions
- Incident response team—tasked with immediate response to an incident to minimize harm to human, tangible, and intangible assets
- Communications and public relations team—tasked with communication with internal and external stakeholders (e.g. families, the community, business partners, the media)
- Recovery team—tasked with dealing with the aftermath of an incident including human assistance and operational recovery
- Systems audit team—tasked with reviewing the program and identifying opportunities for improvement

For teams to be successful, there needs to be a mix of competences, personalities, and representation from different functions and divisions of the organization (e.g. legal, human resources, operations, public relations, safety, security). Where feasible, teams may include representatives from law enforcement and first responders, as well as threat assessment, psychological counseling, safety, and security experts. External experts should be familiar with the local risk environment and context, preventing and managing violence in organizations, and the type of activities the organization engages in.

In smaller organizations, people frequently wear multiple hats and perform multiple functions. Therefore, it may be more efficient to integrate other functions with the system to prevent and manage violence.

Roles, responsibilities, and authorities should be communicated within the organization, as well as to relevant people external to the organization. Organizational charts, job descriptions, and a responsibility matrix are useful tools for communicating responsibilities and authorities internally and externally.

Flexibility should be built into the system. Allocation of resources should consider both the current and future needs of an organization. Develop procedures to track the benefits and costs of the program and related activities. Include costs related to an incident and business continuity. To ensure their adequacy, allocation of resources should be reviewed periodically, ideally in conjunction with the overall management review. In evaluating adequacy of resources, consideration should be given to planned changes in activities, locations, projects, and/or operations.

Resource allocations for the program and teams should consider access to resources for normal and emergency operations.

To ensure transparency, financial and administrative procedures should be established consistent with accepted accounting procedures clearly defining authorizations, responsibilities, and spending limitations. Prior to an incident, define and gather information that will be necessary to file an insurance claim. During and after an incident a clearly defined process to allocate resources and file for insurance will help expedite the response and recovery efforts.

TRAINING, AWARENESS, AND COMPETENCE

Each person from every function in the organization can play a role in preventing and managing violence since anyone can be affected by and have potential impacts on safety and security. Awareness training should recognize that anyone can have good ideas how to improve the system, as well as provide valuable intelligence to identify risks. For example, the maintenance staff frequently sees many aspects of operation. Do they know what to look for and how to report concerns?

Awareness, education, training, and experience contribute to building competence. All persons working on behalf of the organization should receive training tailored to their needs, capabilities, maturity, functions, and activities. Appropriate training targeted to the audience can drive a culture of risk and security awareness. As with many educational programs, repetition, and active engagement help with retention of the learning objectives. Using multiple methods at multiple times both addresses the fact that different people retain information differently, as well as reinforces the importance of the subject within the organization. Top management's participation in training programs also reinforces the importance of the subject within the organization. One-off approaches frequently send the message that top management is simply going through the motions of providing training. Depending on the audience, scare tactics may be counterproductive.

The organization should establish, implement, and maintain training and awareness processes to assure all persons working on their behalf (e.g. employees, staff, and contractors) understand the following:

1. The importance of compliance with the policies, procedures, and practices for managing violence in the organization
2. The significant threats, hazards, and risks, and the impacts associated with their functions and activities, and the security benefits of improved personal performance
3. The roles, responsibilities, and authorities for themselves and others in managing violence in the organization
4. The communication mechanisms for reporting concerns and identifying risks, as well as responding and recovering from an incident
5. Procedures for incident response and management
6. Availability of internal and external assistance programs to prevent, respond to, and recover from violent events
7. Individual rights and obligations (e.g. legal, privacy, information sharing, and documentation)
8. The potential consequences of departure from specified procedures

Persons undertaking work activities that can cause or may result in significant actual or potential threats, hazards, and risks or associated impacts and/or are responsible for responding to incidents should be competent to do so. Once required competencies are identified, the organization should ensure that persons performing these activities have the required competencies.

Safety and security awareness training should reflect the responsibilities related to an individual's activities during normal operations as well as during an incident. It should take into account the audience's existing knowledge and understanding of the subject material. Typical steps in developing safety and security awareness training include the following:

- Identify awareness and training needs
- Define awareness and training objectives and performance metrics
- Design and develop a training plan to address defined training needs and objectives
- Select suitable methods and materials for the target audience
- Provide training of target groups using multiple delivery times and methods
- Document and monitor training delivered
- Evaluate training received against defined competence needs and requirements

- Assess efficacy of training program and identify opportunities for improvement

Integrating safety and security awareness training into recruitment and job training programs helps reinforce the message that safety and security are integral to all the person's activities in the organization. Building retention of information and competence is a primary objective. Effective programs build "muscle memory" (engraining a specific task into memory through repetition), so an appropriate response becomes a more natural response.

Appropriately designed exercises and drills are excellent learning tools that help build muscle

---

Training to promote cultural change

Cultural change to promote security and risk awareness is about people. Plans and programs need to be dynamic and "alive." Ongoing training and awareness are essential. The question you need to answer is how best to communicate the messages of the plans and procedures to your people. Otherwise, the only question you will be asking is whether the reports, plans, and procedures should sit on the shelf vertically or horizontally.

---

memory. Care must be taken to tailor exercises and drills to the target audience to promote retention of information. Many people retain information better through entertaining learning methods than through scare tactics. Methods that build stress may actually send a message of fear and hopelessness. Therefore, develop a safety and security awareness training approach that helps build a sense of empowerment and personal responsibility.

COMMUNICATION MECHANISMS AND WARNINGS

Effective communication requires mechanisms for two-way flow of information top-down, bottom-up, and across functional lines. Since persons working on behalf of the organization are its eyes and ears, they can be an excellent source of information, issues, concerns, and ideas. Workplace violence and targeted violence frequently are preceded by warning signs shared with family and friends. Therefore, communications and warning mechanism should include information flow to and from relevant external parties.

Communications and warning procedures and processes should consider the following:

- Internal communication mechanisms between the various levels and functions of the organization and with partner entities
- Receiving, documenting, and responding to relevant communication from internal and external parties
- Emergency warnings and required actions prior to, during, and after an incident within the organization
- Facilitation of structured communication with law enforcement and other first responders
- Consistent, accurate, and timely messaging with the media, community, and impacted persons during and after an event
- Availability of the communication mechanisms during a crisis situation
- Mechanisms for feedback on program efficacy and opportunities for improvement

A variety of communication methods are available and should be deployed. Examples include minutes of meetings, bulletin board postings, newsletters, suggestion boxes/schemes, complaints and whistleblower mechanisms, websites, e-mail, meetings, workshops, and joint committees. Integrating a discussion of the risk of violence into regular business and staff meetings reinforces that safety and security management is an integral part of every activity. Both identified and anonymous mechanisms to express concerns are helpful but are only effective if coupled with analysis, action, and feedback processes.

The organization should establish, implement, and maintain procedures for receiving, documenting, and responding to relevant communication from external parties. The organization should also have in place a process for communicating with external parties in case of emergency situations or incidents that could affect or concern them.

For both internal and external communication, it is important that information should be

- Understandable, adequately explained, and tailored to the target audience
- Relevant to the audience's interests and concerns
- Traceable with sources documented
- Accurate and timely

- Respectful of people's rights and privacy
- Vetted to assure it cannot be exploited by an adversary or misused on social media

Effective communication is one of the most important ingredients in preparation, response to, and recovery from a violent event. Internal and external stakeholders should be identified in order to convey alerts, warnings, crisis, and organizational response information. Consider communications strategies for families, neighbors, community groups and other interested groups, local officials, law enforcement, regulatory agencies, and emergency responders. It may be appropriate to segment the audiences to tailor messages specifically for a group. Determine which methods are appropriate for communications and warnings. Evaluate and periodically determine the effectiveness of the communications process.

Preplanning for communications is highly beneficial. Draft message templates, scripts, and statements in advance based on threats identified in the risk assessment. Establish procedures to ensure that communications can be distributed at short notice, particularly those related to incident response.

Communications are particularly crucial when emergencies occur. Concerned and impacted parties, as well as the media, will ask questions related to the emergency. Confusing and contradictory information will result in mistrust and fear. Therefore, a key objective is to avoid misinformation and room for misinterpretation. Be honest and avoid sugarcoating, embellishing, or speculating. If you do not know an answer, state that you are still assessing the situation and focused on the well-being of your people. Communicating a concern that your top priority is accounting for your people and that their health and safety precedes material concerns.

Proactive communications

Teams should coordinate their functions with law enforcement and first responders. You have to develop a relationship well before an incident occurs. Interfacing and information sharing should be proactively developed before it is needed in an emergency. Your incident management team will be the immediate responders, and they must know how to coordinate their activities with law enforcement and other first responders.

The organization should designate a single primary spokesperson, and backups who will manage and disseminate communications to the media and others during an incident. This individual should be trained in media relations prior to an event. All information should be funneled through a single source to assure that the messages being delivered are consistent. Persons working on behalf of the organization should be informed where to refer calls from the media and that only authorized organization spokespeople are authorized to speak to the media.

DOCUMENTATION AND DOCUMENT CONTROL

To ensure that its system of management, policies, and procedures are understood and operating effectively, an organization should develop and maintain adequate documentation. The purpose of such documentation is to provide necessary information to persons working on its behalf and other relevant parties. Documentation should be collected and maintained in a way that reflects the culture and needs of an organization, building upon its existing information system. The extent of the documentation can differ from one organization to another but it should describe the policies and procedures that need to be implemented in a consistent fashion. When processes for managing violence are aligned with other processes, it is frequently more efficient for the organization to combine relevant documentation.

Records, which provide information on results achieved or evidence of activities performed, are an important part of an organization's documentation. Record maintenance should be coordinated with legal counsel to assure their integrity and meet the legal and litigation needs of the organization. Information security and privacy protection should be major considerations of any document and record maintenance system.

Records should be reviewed during the management review process. Examples of records include the following:

- Risk and threat assessment documentation (e.g. register/catalog of identified risks)
- Information required for insurance coverage and claims
- Security, threat, and vulnerability surveys
- Grievance, complaints, whistleblower reports, and suggestions with investigation reports
- Investigation reports of threat assessment team
- Background screening and vetting documentation
- Documentation required by regulatory agencies

59

- Training records
- Exercise, drill, and audit reports
- Incident reports
- Law enforcement reports

To ensure that everyone is working with the proper documents, the organization should have a clearly defined procedure for document control. Implementation of this procedure should ensure that

- Documents are cataloged and can be located.
- Documents can be identified with the appropriate organization, division, function, activity, or contact person.
- Documents (other than records) are regularly reviewed, revised as necessary, and approved by authorized personnel prior to issue.
- The current versions of relevant documents are available at all locations where activities are conducted.
- Obsolete documents are promptly removed from all points of issue and use and archived according to the legal and liability needs of the organization.

Documentation and document control are tools to help the organization better manage information. They are not an end in and of themselves. Therefore, keep documentation simple and aligned with the culture and other information dissemination practices of the organization.

OPERATIONAL CONTROLS AND PROCEDURES

Develop procedures for controlling activities and operations that are associated with risks. Ensure that persons working on behalf of the organization are trained on the procedures. Procedures should cover both normal and abnormal operating conditions, particularly risks associated with potential violence. Documenting your procedures avoids ambiguities and leads to more consistent performance.

Integrating the management of violence into the standard operating procedures (SOPs) of the organization increases security and risk awareness. It sends a clear message that safety and security are integral parts of all the organization's activities. In addition to integrating security and risk awareness into SOPs for normal activities, there will be a need to develop operating procedures and controls for the system of management to prevent and manage violence in the organization. Specific controls and procedures associated with the system of management should include procedures for the following:

- Code of ethics and professionalism
- Employee and contractor background screening and vetting
- Mechanisms to report risks and persons of concern, as well as suspicious objects
- Complaints and/or whistleblower mechanisms
- Suggestion mechanisms for identifying risks and potential improvements
- Mechanisms to assess and act on reports of persons and issues of concern
- Conflict resolution mechanisms
- Cyber security, online, and social media practices (including online harassment and bullying)
- Physical security measures (access controls, locks, alarms, surveillance)
- Access to support mechanisms and employee assistance programs for victims and impacted persons including pre- and post-incident resources
- Response to violence
- Reporting and documenting violence
- Investigation of violence and remediation actions
- Training programs

Most organizations have either formal or informal SOPs describing the normal activities and functions it conducts. Many of these activities and functions have associated risks. Review the SOPs and update them by including the following questions related to preventing and managing violence in the organization:

1. What are the risk and threats associated with the activity and function described in the SOP?
2. Who are the internal stakeholders who can impact and be impacted by the identified risks and threats?
3. Who are the external stakeholders who can impact and be impacted by the identified risks and threats?
4. Are there indicators to look for that the risk may manifest?
5. What would be the consequences of the identified risks and threats manifesting themselves?

6. What are the current control measures to manage the risks and threats?
7. Are the current control measures adequate and can they be improved?

By updating the SOPs addressing these questions, followed by awareness training for the persons conducting the SOP, it is possible to ingrain security and risk awareness in the activity, increasing the likelihood that the risk can be lowered. This also helps promote an awareness of warning signs that something may be amiss with the activity described in the SOP.

To make your SOPs actionable, risks, roles, responsibilities, authorities, and resources should be defined, documented, and communicated. Also, consider the competence needed to implement the procedures and if there is need for additional training. Operational controls and procedures should be part of the business review cycle to determine if they are effective and if there are opportunities for improvement.

HUMAN RESOURCE MANAGEMENT

Enhancing human resource management plays a major role in preventing and managing violence in the organization. Some human resource topics to consider on how to improve safety and security of people working on behalf of the organization include the following:

- Selection, screening, and vetting of personnel
- Selection, screening, and vetting of subcontractors and outsource partners
- Orientation and ongoing training on policies, procedures, and the code of ethics
- Employee assistance programs, including access the mental health and counseling services
- Internal reporting mechanisms (e.g. tip and suggestion boxes, complaint, grievance, and whistleblower mechanisms)
- External reporting mechanisms (for family, partners, friends, and community members)
- Medical and insurance policies to address consequences of an incident
- Post-incident support, including leave, bereavement, and alternative work location policies
- Job tasking and placement of individuals

Procedures for these topics should be established, documented, and consistently implemented. Clear criteria should be established which are fairly applied to all personnel, subcontractors, and outsource partners. Procedures should be reviewed for compliance with legal, regulatory, and contractual requirements, particularly privacy requirements. Records from these procedures should protect sensitive information and be maintained consistent with the jurisdictional requirements of the work location.

Vetting may include reviews of criminal and domestic violence history, evaluation for substance abuse, and physical and mental assessment of fitness for duties. Note that requesting and access to this information may be controlled by jurisdictional laws and requirements.

To be effective, reporting mechanisms need to include a clearly defined hierarchical process for receiving, investigating, resolving, and remediating reported issues and suggestions. Whenever possible, a root cause analysis should be conducted to identify corrective and preventive actions needed to avoid a recurrence of the issue. Documenting the outcomes of the investigation with appropriate feedback loops demonstrates that the reported issues were duly investigated and acted upon.

Employee assistance programs not only provide an avenue for individuals to express concerns and seek help, they reinforce the message that safety and security are top priorities for the organization. Not only do they provide a venue for potential victims to seek help, but they also provide a way for troubled individuals who could have potential problems to seek help.

INCIDENT MANAGEMENT

The possibility of an act of violence occurring exists for any type, size, and location of organization. "It can't happen here" and other forms of denial are an

---

Beware of sensationalism

It is important to keep your eye on the obligation of keeping people safe and secure. All organizations have limited resources and time. Sensationalism in the media may distort the perception of the threat. You need to prepare for both the potential day-to-day acts of violence and the rare chance of a terroristic or active assailant event. Focusing the bulk of your resources on rare events may not be the most prudent use of resources and may leave people exposed to more common occurrences. What measures can you implement to minimize both likelihood and consequences for either day-to-day or rare events?

---

irresponsible approach to management. The likelihood that an active shooter event or terrorist attack will directly impact your organization may be extremely small, but the consequences of one of these events will almost always be very significant, so you need a plan to be prepared.

An organization should establish, implement, and maintain procedures detailing how to identify potential violent acts and emergency situations that can have adverse impacts. It needs to develop plans for appropriate prevention, mitigation, response, and recovery actions for such situations. Effective preparation and response can reduce injuries, prevent or minimize incidents and impacts, protect people internal and external to the organization, reduce asset losses, and minimize downtime.

Many organizations already have incident management and/or emergency action plans for fire, natural disasters, and work-related accidents. Many of the concepts and actions needed to prevent and manage violence in the organization may already be described in these incident management and/or emergency action plans. These plans typically address warnings, evacuations, shelter-in-place, assembly areas, drills, notifications, and coordination with public officials. Therefore, the first step in developing the plans to manage a violent event is to review the existing incident management and/or emergency action plans to see what can be leveraged. One of the big differences between managing fire, natural disasters, and work-related accident events and violent events is that the latter is caused by humans; therefore, a malevolent act includes elements of planning and improvisation by the adversary. A human can observe and identify soft targets and then modify an attack accordingly; the other forms of emergencies do not have this inherent flexibility. For example, an assailant may be aware of evacuation routes and assembly areas, planning a secondary attack when evacuation procedures begin.

Effective incident and emergency action plans should include procedures for

- Assessing the potential for an incident including indicators and warning signs
- Measures for acting on indicators and notifying the threat assessment team
- Internal and external communications protocols before, during, and after an incident, including methods for maintaining communications during an emergency

- Measures for preventing incidents, preparedness, and preemptive impact mitigation including maintenance of emergency response equipment
- Measures for assessing the situation and initiating a response, including mobilization of the incident response team and appropriate resources
- Plans and procedures for responding to incidents
- Triage and immediate first aid and victim care
- Methods for promoting awareness and periodically testing the plans and procedures
- Measures to minimize the impacts of the incident
- Business continuity management
- Provisions for family assistance, emergency support, health and medical support, post-incident counseling, and community mass casualty plans
- Recovery measures
- Post-incident review and after-action planning
- Documentation and information management

A cross-functional team should develop the incident and emergency action plans. Representatives from engineering, process management, human resources, environment, health and safety, and maintenance can provide valuable input when asked "what if" questions related to the organization's activities and functions. All impacted persons (e.g. employees, temporary workers, suppliers, property owners, tenants, contractors, visitors) need to know what to do during an incident which could escalate into an emergency situation. Consideration should be given to normal and abnormal operating conditions, as well as persons with special neeeds.

Many organizations already have business continuity plans for response to and recovery from disruptive events (e.g. natural disasters, infrastructure failures, accidents, intentional actions). The incident management plans for managing violence should be integrated with the organization's business continuity plans. Given the traumatic nature of violence, particular attention should be paid to human factors such as post-incident stress and recovery from the trauma caused by a violent event.

There is no boilerplate approach to effective incident and emergency action plans. Plans must be tailored to the audience that will need to implement the procedures. Consider how the people associated with your organization will respond in a stressful situation and tailor plans accordingly. For example, planning for an elementary school will differ from planning for a secondary school. People tagged to perform leadership functions on the incident response team need to be able to cope with the stress of an enfolding event if they are to be effective. Can they lead under stress?

Incident and emergency action plans can either gather dust or gather momentum. Emergency situations typically do not unfold exactly as anticipated. Also, people often respond differently under stress than they might in a passive environment. Therefore, periodic testing of emergency plans and procedures is essential to build the awareness for impacted persons to be able to assess their situation and improvise their response based on how the incident is developing. People need to understand the parameters of response, as well as understand they may need to adapt during an actual event.

8

Building the Framework— Checking and Evaluation

Checking involves measurement, monitoring, and evaluation of the performance of the organization's system for preventing and managing violence. The process seeks to proactively identify weaknesses and nonconformities in the system of management's plans and procedures enabling it to take corrective actions before an incident takes place. Evaluating and testing plans and procedures provides information needed to make improvements. Keeping records of performance assessments provides a basis for demonstrating an appropriate duty of care, as well as provides data for comparing measures to reduce risk. It gives the organization a reliable source of information on day-to-day operations and results of its efforts to prevent and manage violence in the organization. Periodic audits of the entire system of management help the organization verify that the system is designed and operating according to plan.

MONITORING AND EVALUATION

The organization should develop procedures for measuring and monitoring its performance on a regular basis. Measurements can be either qualitative or quantitative. Consider what can be measured and what is the most useful information to assess performance and identify opportunities for improvement. Monitoring and measurement should identify both successes and areas in need of correction and improvement. The monitoring and measurement process should also evaluate if the organization is meeting its compliance, legal, and contractual obligations.

The risk environment can be very dynamic. Therefore, the organization should conduct ongoing monitoring of the risk environment establishing triggers for action if conditions that will impact its ability to manage risks of violence change. As new risks emerge, the organization should review its risk control measures to determine if they are adequate or if they need to be adapted to the changing conditions.

The frequency and methodology for the evaluation processes

"If you can't measure it, you can't improve it." Peter Drucker

Unfortunately, not everything can be quantified directly by some kind of hard metric. This is particularly true in security where it is difficult to measure "nothing happening" when events are rare. Improved performance may be linked to decreased turnover and absenteeism rates, and/or increased productivity, workers' sense of well-being and confidence, improved morale, loyalty to the organization, and creation of a community. Consider qualitative and indirect measures in evaluations.

will depend on the organization's size, type, and complexity. Frequency can be affected by past performance or legal and contractual requirements. It can be beneficial to integrate the evaluation process with management system audits; health, environmental, and safety assessments; physical and cyber security surveys; and/or quality assurance checks. To obtain a different perspective, it may be worth considering periodically conducting an independent review using external auditors. A different set of eyes helps identify issues that might have been overlooked or not even considered. Records of these evaluations should be maintained to demonstrate appropriate due diligence.

The outcome of an activity or process can be impacted by a number of factors. By conducting a process-mapping exercise, it is possible to determine what the key factors are and how to measure them. Metrics should be based on both process and outcome measurements. Process metrics look at the performance of the processes to control risk and if operational controls are being implemented correctly (e.g. the number of persons trained and demonstrating competence on a control measure). Outcome metrics look at the results of activities, processes, and actions. Performance indicators should be tied to the organization's objectives and targets, and the risk assessment, as well as provide information about the efficacy of the program.

TESTING THE SYSTEM—EXERCISES AND DRILLS

Drills and exercises test and validate the system of management, plans, and capabilities. They examine if the program is operating as planned, detect capability gaps, and identify areas for improvement. They are also an excellent method for promoting awareness and reducing response times during an incident. Few people can think clearly, calmly, and logically during the height of stress in a crisis. So, it is important to test your procedures before an event takes place rather than hope they will work under stress of an incident. Similar to fire and natural disaster drills, periodic evacuation drills will help people understand shelter-in-place, escape routes, and assembly points.

Exercises and drills test the appropriateness and effectiveness of risk treatment plans, processes, and procedures to prevent and manage violence in the organization. Scenarios for exercises and drills should be based on issues that were identified in the risk and threat assessment process. Tests should be designed to educate people and not scare and intimidate them. They help build team readiness and identifying leaders who can operate under stress. An exercise or drill will help people be effective in their duties to manage violence, clarify their roles, and identify areas for improvement in the system.

Technology solutions that were deployed should also be regularly tested (e.g. alarms, detectors, surveillance equipment, communications systems). Alarms, warnings, and communications systems are particularly important to test to determine if they indeed have the capacity to operate properly during an emergency. Equipment and technologies might not operate as assumed when people are under stress. Therefore, it is important to test if the alarms, warnings, and communication systems will operate as expected and people understand what their response is supposed to be by conducting realistic scenarios.

Start with simple exercises and drills with clearly defined scope, objectives, and outcomes to test. As the exercise program matures, and based on the organization's resources and experience, the complexity and realism of the exercises can be increased. Focus on making the exercise a learning and awareness experience for the participants. It is important that all persons working on behalf of the organization participate, including management personnel. Top management should lead by example and exhibit a commitment to participate and review the outcomes of exercises and drills. Weaknesses should be corrected expeditiously.

Designing exercises and drills involves a careful balance of objectives, frequency, and methods. They must be tailored to the target audience when determining appropriate methods, complexity, and stress levels. People need to feel they learnt something from the exercise. Poorly designed exercises may result in complacency, desensitization, and disinterest. Unless participation is mandatory, a mind-set may develop that exercises are a nuisance and people may begin to ignore warning signals. Debriefs should include not only an evaluation of the safety and security procedures tested but also should critique the exercise and drill. Improvements should be implemented so that people see the value in the exercise. A formal exercise report should be generated which can be reviewed for future exercise planning as well as reviewed by top management in systems review.

Once the scope of the exercise is defined, all impacted persons should be considered for inclusion (e.g. employees, temporary workers, contractors, building owners, tenants). Law enforcement and first responders should be included when practical. This is an excellent opportunity to determine law enforcement and first responder response times if an incident should occur, as well as to coordinate response actions between the internal incident management team and the external responders. Also, consider involvement of neighbors and the larger community when either the organization or external interested parties would benefit from participation and knowledge of the outcomes. However, consider if involvement of outsiders will in itself pose unnecessary risks.

SYSTEM AUDITS

The system audit gages whether the system of management for violence prevention and management in the organization is living up to expectations and performing as planned. It helps determine if policies and procedures have been properly implemented and are effective and efficient. Audits may be conducted using a phased approach or as a single comprehensive audit based on the organization's resources, capabilities, and the need not to disrupt normal activities. The audits should be conducted on a periodic basis, optimally linked to the normal business review cycle.

Audits may be performed by internal or external personnel. The key factor is that people should not audit their own work and the processes they designed or are tasked with executing. Auditors should be impartial and objective. Audits should be providing an "other-eyes-on" perspective of system efficacy. The audit report should identify weaknesses, areas of nonconformance, areas of concern, and opportunities for improvement, as well as provide input to overall system review by management.

9

Building the Framework— Review and Improvement

Building the framework is not a one-off activity. The framework is a management tool to help the organization better prevent, respond to, and recover from an act of violence. Establishing a cycle of management review is an essential element for continually improving the system. It also reinforces the message that the system is a dynamic part of all organizational activities. Integrating the review cycle for preventing and managing violence into the normal business review cycle will help promote seamless integration of violence management into all the organization's activities and functions.

Top management as well as representatives from appropriate functions in the organization should participate in the review process. The review should consider how the measures for managing violence are helping to improve overall performance and the organization's ability to provide value through the creation of products and services. The review should evaluate the system's continuing suitability, adequacy, and effectiveness.

Inputs to the management review may include the following:

- Evaluations of system of management performance
- Evaluation of compliance with applicable legal, regulatory, and contractual requirements
- Results of the threat and risk assessments
- Performance of security and safety measures to prevent, respond to, and recover from violent acts

- Results of exercises, drills, and audits
- Reports from employee assistance programs
- Communications from internal parties, including suggestions, tips, concerns, and complaints
- Communication from external parties, including expressions of concern and complaints
- Assessment of the extent to which objectives and targets have been met
- Status of corrective and preventive actions
- Follow-up actions from previous management reviews
- Changes in the threat and risk profile, including public warnings
- Changes in legal, regulatory, and contractual requirements, as well as liability concerns
- Adequacy and appropriateness of performance metrics
- Reports and lessons learned from incidents and near misses
- Root cause analysis of identified problems

Outputs from the review may include decisions on the following:

- The system of management's suitability, adequacy, and effectiveness
- Changes to financial, human, and physical resources
- Improvements and modifications needed for procedures and risk controls
- Changes needed to promote a culture of risk and threat awareness
- Changes needed to better integrate the system of management to prevent and manage violence into the overall system of management
- Actions required related to changes to policy, objectives, targets, and other elements of the system of management

The identification of actual and potential system weaknesses and nonconformities provides an opportunity for improvement. An organization should understand why weaknesses and nonconformities exist. This can be achieved by analyzing the root causes. Corrective actions which address the immediate problem should be coupled with preventive actions, or changes to prevent a recurrence. When opportunities for improvement are identified, they should be evaluated to determine what specific actions can be taken. The actions for improvement should be planned and assessed to determine if they are changing or introducing new risks. Improvements can also be identified by benchmarking against best practices of similar organizations. Improvements need not take place in all areas simultaneously.

When considering opportunities for improvement, the organization should consider the culture and methods for change management in the organization. The timing and approach may be influenced by the size, type, and culture of the organization.

The framework is a never-ending spiral moving upward toward heightened performance. The organization continues to build the resilience of the organization and the people who impact and can be impacted by its activities and functions. Start with low-hanging fruit and build momentum to address more complex issues as the framework matures.

Section III

Tactics and Control Measures

10

Policy Statement

The policy statement sets the tone for preventing and managing violence in the organization. It should reflect the organization's and top management's commitment to prevent violence, when possible, and maintain a safe and secure environment at all times. The example policy statement can be used as a starting point template for top management of the organization to tailor a policy statement to their needs. Once completed, the policy statement should be visibly endorsed by management and communicated to all persons working on the organization's behalf, as well as posted on its website.

Note that many jurisdictions require by-laws or regulations that employers maintain a reasonably safe, secure, and healthy work environment. A policy statement is the first step in meeting this obligation. This generic policy statement can be used as a reference, but the organization's policy statement should be aligned with jurisdictional laws and regulations.

Below is a generic policy statement. The policy statement should be dated and signed by the authorizing person from top management of the organization (preferably president or chief executive officer). In the example below, input the name of your organization as indicated by italics.

Prevention and Management of Violence Policy Statement

(Name of Organization)

(Date)

OBJECTIVE

(Name of Organization) recognizes its obligation to promote a safe, secure, and healthy environment for persons working on its behalf. This policy represents a commitment of management and all persons working on our behalf to work in unison to provide an environment free from violence, threats of violence, harassment, intimidation, and other threatening or aggressive behavior in all work-related activities, on-site and off-site. We will work together to create a safe environment where mutual respect is extended to all.

SCOPE

This policy outlines responsibilities of all persons working on behalf of *(Name of Organization)* (management, full-time and part-time employees, temporary personal, and subcontractors) to prevent and manage violence in all the organization's activities and functions. This policy applies equally to all persons working on behalf of *(Name of Organization)*. This policy covers workplace violence associated with day-to-day activities, as well as targeted violence associated with active shooters/assailants, terroristic acts, and other forms of random violence related to the organization's activities.

Violence may take the form of physical acts of violence or threats to harm a person or assets (tangible and intangible). Harassment, intimidation, and other abusive behaviors, whether verbal or electronic, psychological or physical, are considered acts of violence. Sexual abuse and harassment is any unwelcome verbal or physical assault or degrading behavior and is considered an act of violence.

MANAGEMENT COMMITMENT

The management of *(Name of Organization)* is committed to the safety and security of all persons working on our behalf. We are committed

78

to providing an environment free from violence, threats of violence, harassment, intimidation, and other disruptive behavior. The management of (*Name of Organization*) is responsible for ensuring the establishment of a system of management to prevent and manage violence in our organization. Safety and security policies and procedures shall be clearly communicated and understood by all persons working on our behalf. All managers and supervisors will enforce the rules fairly and uniformly. We will provide adequate authority and budgetary resources to meet our goals and responsibilities for maintaining a safe and secure work environment, including establishing and supporting programs to assist persons working on our behalf to address potential and actual issues related to violence originating in or being brought to our organization.

EXPECTED CONDUCT

All persons working on behalf of (*Name of Organization*) are expected to understand and comply with this policy. All persons working on our behalf are required to respect legal obligations and the rights and dignity of others and display mutual courtesy as well as engage in safe and appropriate behavior in all activities related to their association with our organization. Respect for others extends to customers, clients, vendors, and visitors. Persons working on behalf of our organization are responsible for their own behavior.

It may not always be possible to predict violent acts; therefore, we ask all persons working on behalf of (*Name of Organization*) to be vigilant. Report any concerns or violent acts to the Threat Assessment Team as soon as possible, providing as much detail as possible. Safety and security concerns should be reported to appropriate authorities rather than addressed through personal intervention. Persons working on behalf of the organizations are expected to fully cooperate with investigations and assessments of potential and actual acts of violence.

Persons working on behalf of (*Name of Organization*) are expected to report to the Threat Assessment Team any protective or restraining orders that include any facility of the organization. They are also encouraged to report to the Threat Assessment Team any safety concerns related to domestic or intimate partner violence. Reports will be treated with appropriate confidentiality.

PROHIBITED CONDUCT

(*Name of Organization*) expects all persons working on its behalf (management, full-time and part-time employees, temporary personal, and subcontractors) to exhibit safe and appropriate behavior in all organization-related activities. Prohibited conduct includes, but is not limited to, the following:

- Injuring another person physically or mentally
- Threatening to injure another person including by direct, indirect, or electronic means—verbal or written
- Threatening to damage tangible and/or intangible assets (property, equipment, reputation, brand)
- Engaging in belligerent, bullying, harassing, intimidating, or other inappropriate and aggressive behavior
- Engaging in coercive, argumentative behavior, horseplay, or fighting that mocks, intimidates, or threatens others
- Creating a potential or actual reasonable fear of injury to another person
- Using abusive or vulgar language toward another person
- Using the organization's resources (physical or electronic) to threaten, harass, intimidate, or stalk others
- Using the organization's resources (physical or electronic) to engage in unauthorized and unlawful activities (including possession, carrying, or transporting drugs)
- Engaging in unauthorized intervention putting oneself or others in harm's way
- Committing inappropriate acts related to domestic or intimate partner violence
- Harassment of a sexual nature (e.g. unwelcome sexual advances, requests for sexual favors, and other verbal, nonverbal, or physical conduct of a sexual nature)
- Possessing, brandishing, or using any weapon (e.g. knife, firearm, explosives, or munitions) while engaged in organizational activities and services if not explicitly preapproved by an appropriate authority
- Violating a restraining order, order of protection, injunction against harassment, or other court order

Courtesy and respect should be extended to all human interactions related to the activities, functions, and services of (*Name of Organization*). Any behavior that is in violation of the above guidelines will be subject to investigation and proportional disciplinary action (including potential dismissal).

GRIEVANCE, WHISTLEBLOWER, AND SUGGESTION PROCEDURE

The management of (*Name of Organization*) is responsible to implement and maintain policies and procedural mechanisms for reporting potential and actual acts of violence. The grievance, whistleblower, and suggestion mechanisms will be free of discrimination. Any person working on behalf of (*Name of Organization*) who witnesses or suspects violence, or are victims of violence, is expected to immediately report such concerns to appropriate management and/or the Threat Assessment Team to avoid escalation of the situation. (*Name of Organization*) will not retaliate against any individual making a good-faith report of potential or actual violence, persons of concern, and/or suspicious activities or objects.

INVESTIGATIONS AND DISCIPLINARY ACTION

The management of (*Name of Organization*) will investigate all reports of threats and actual incidents of violence expeditiously and discreetly. Investigations will be conducted by impartial and competent investigators. Criteria for preventing and managing violence will be applied fairly and equitably for all persons working on our behalf. (*Name of Organization*) reserves the right to suspend persons working on its behalf, with or without pay, pending the investigation into potential or actual violence.

Persons found in violation of this policy or procedures to prevent and manage violence, including threats of or actual violence, will be subject to prompt and proportional disciplinary action. Disciplinary actions may include reassignment, demotion, financial actions, and/or termination of the relationship with our organization.

CONFIDENTIALITY

(*Name of Organization*) will make every effort to respect privacy and keep reports confidential. Personal information will be kept as confidential as possible, except where there is a legal requirement of disclosure and/or the "need to know" to protect people or resolve an issue.

11

Teams, Roles, Responsibilities, and Authorities

For any program in an organization to prevent and manage violence, it is essential to be inclusive. Assume that violence can impact any and all persons working on behalf of the organization. When developing plans to manage the risk of violence, it is important to keep in mind that everyone is part of the risk equation; therefore, everyone has a role to play. While an individual may be tasked with championing and overseeing the program, it is important not to send the message that they are solely responsible for the safety and well-being of all individuals. Rather, it is important to emphasize personal responsibility and awareness for oneself and their colleagues.

Management commitment and diverse worker involvement are key to establishing a successful and effective program. Persons working on behalf of the organization should be aware of their roles and the importance of the following:

- Treating all persons encountered in the workplace with respect and dignity
- Compliance with the workplace violence policy and measures to prevent, minimize, and respond to acts of violence
- Proactively engaging in violence prevention program and understanding the need to be aware and use the complaints, whistleblower, and suggestions mechanisms to alert designated persons of potential issues

- Reporting violent incidents, no matter the nature, expeditiously and accurately
- Participating in awareness and training programs, as well as drills and exercises

Management should emphasize the need for risk awareness and its commitment to the program to manage violence in the organization. Management's mantra needs to be that inputs from all persons working on behalf of the organization are welcome and that information that is shared will be investigated while protecting the privacy and dignity of persons involved. Management should demonstrate this commitment by

- Understanding how violence impacts the achievement of strategic, tactical, operational, and reputational objectives.
- Establishing, implementing, and reviewing the workplace violence policy.
- Including management of violence as an integral part of regular business meetings and organizational planning.
- Providing the necessary resources (financial and human) needed to achieve the objectives of the program. This includes designating the appropriate responsibilities and authorities for the program.
- Leading by example—by practicing what they preach, management demonstrates the importance of the program.
- Establishing employee assistance and support programs.
- Assuring that necessary teams are established, staffed with competent individuals, and provided adequate resources to support the program to manage violence.
- Establishing feedback and communication mechanisms to enable prevention, response, and recovery from potential violent events, including a commitment to expeditiously and fairly address issues.
- Maintaining a transparent and fair system of investigation and accountability for violence.
- Monitoring, reviewing, and improving the program to manage violence in the organization.

In addition, the human resource management team should

- Implement a system of background screening and vetting that minimizes the likelihood of potential violent events.
- Assure that organizational policy, laws, and regulations are consistently enforced in all human resource management functions.

- Provide awareness training for new hires as well as on regular intervals.
- Maintain timely, fair, and transparent communications and reporting mechanisms.
- Provide persons working on behalf of the organization with truthful and regular performance evaluations to avoid surprises.
- Receive and investigate, in a timely fashion, concerns about health, safety, and security.
- Explore de-escalation measures, including those to reduce stress in the work environment.

Regardless of an individual's role within an organization, every person at every level needs to understand the following:

- They are a risk-maker and risk-taker; therefore, a risk manager (particularly, how their activities in the organization impact the risk profile).
- They have an obligation to treat all others with which they interact with dignity and respect.
- An "it can't happen here" mentality is not acceptable; violence may occur regardless of type, size, and activities of any organization.
- Personal awareness and responsibility are everyone's obligation.
- Prevention is top objective of the program to manage violence; therefore, everyone should familiarize themselves with indicators of enhanced risk as well as measures and methods to avoid an incident.
- Identification of the steps and measures the individual needs to take to survive an incident and help others survive.
- How an individual interfaces with immediate and first responders during an incident.

Different people working on behalf of the organization will have different competencies as well as different capabilities in managing stress. The following subsections describe teams that should be established to support the system of preventing and managing violence in the organization. Depending on the resources, size, and nature of the organization, these may be discrete teams, teams with shared members, or a single team with multiple functions. The most important factor is to have a diverse group of people representing the breath of activities and people within the organization, who have been provided adequate training to be competent in the tasks assigned to the team. Not all team members need every competence required of the team; however, the team's overall competence should be assessed against the competencies needed by the team. As described below, the one team that is best as a stand-alone team is the management system auditing team.

THREAT ASSESSMENT TEAM

A team should be established that is tasked with assessing and managing risks and threats related to potential violence in the organization. An individual should be designated team leader who commands the respect (and ear) of both management and fellow workers. The team leader will interface with the human resources department and management, be the point of contact for communicating with internal and external stakeholders, determine competencies and expertise needed for the threat assessment team, designate roles and any subteams in the team, lead investigations, and prepare threat assessment team reports.

Team members should be drawn from top management; workers' representatives or labor organizers; human resources management staff; health, safety, and security staff; operations managers and engineers; legal department; and maintenance department and other support staff (this last group is frequently overlooked; however, it is a group that can identify issues in a variety of day-to-day activities). External experts in security, psychology, and/or emergency response may be considered where in-house expertise is not available. In addition to diversity of roles in the operations of the organization, the team should exhibit diversity in experience, skills, temperament and personality, and perspectives. Violence in organizations is a people-oriented issue; therefore, team members should be as fair and free of bias as possible (all people have some biases, so these should be identified), exhibit empathy toward other individuals, communicate well, and be able to bring a range of perspectives to the team. Teams that lack a range of perspective sometimes drop into the pitfall of groupthink and group bias.

When picking team members (this task may fall on the team leader in concert with top management or human resource management), start by assessing the competencies and perspectives needed to achieve the objectives of the team. Through the team selection process and competence building training, the team should be able to address the range of issues associated with potential violence in the organization.

Example of the need for inclusion

A hospital in a high-risk area was having an ongoing problem of assaults on its nursing staff that was seriously affecting the provision of medical services. The chief security officer (CSO) was tasked with finding a solution. Based on his military, police, and security experience, he devised a technology solution. While the number of assaults diminished slightly, the associated negative effects on the provision of medical services remained unchanged due to an ongoing fear of assault. Over the objections of the CSO, a threat assessment team was created that included administrators, nurses, doctors, and labor union representatives. The threat assessment team surveyed healthcare staff that articulated exactly what their safety and security concerns were and their perceived needs to address the security, safety, and healthcare issues. A new solution was devised which included a role for healthcare staff, an integrated approach to technology and physical security, and risk awareness training. The result was an improvement in provision of medical services, improved worker morale (coupled with increased productivity), and the introduction of "risk-thinking" among hospital staff that used this approach to identify and solve other non-security-related problems.

Not all expertise may be available in-house. Determine what competencies may be lacking and seek external assistance. There are local and national government programs in different localities that can provide assistance in addressing issues related to violence in organizations. Furthermore, emergency management and first responder communities can be valuable resources to support the threat assessment team. Legal advice, particularly understanding jurisdictional criminal, labor, and privacy laws, is essential. Either someone familiar with these aspects of law from the legal department or external expertise should be included in the threat assessment team. Many organizations may not have in-house health, safety, and security personnel. In these cases, it is very helpful to seek the services of professional service providers to provide input; however, outsourcing the program to prevent and manage violence may result in a sense of outsourcing the internal responsibilities essential for program success.

The threat assessment team will work closely with the human resources department, as well as with safety, security, business continuity, and environmental protection officers to develop and implement the system of management to prevent and manage violence. Depending on the management style of the organization, these different groups may take the lead in certain tasks. As long as all tasks are covered and coordinated, exact roles and responsibilities should be assigned based on the overall management system of the organization. This will help integrate the violence prevention and management measures into all day-to-day activities of the organization.

The threat assessment team's first step should be to clearly define and verify its scope and parameters of operation, as well as assuring that it has the necessary authorities and resources to effectively carry out its mandate. This should be followed by developing the policies, processes, and procedures it will use to assure consistent, transparent, and fair methods of operation. This should include procedures for the following:

1. Roles, responsibilities, and authorities in the team including division of functions (e.g. what functions are within the scope of the threat assessment team and which should be referred to human resources, safety, or security divisions)
2. Risk and threat assessment methodology
3. Monitoring the risk environment, individuals, and behaviors
4. Communications protocols for receiving and disseminating information including reporting procedures for persons working on behalf of the organization
5. Chronology of actions to be taken in light of a threat and/or reported concern
6. Investigation protocols
7. Information, data, and report handling, including confidentiality, privacy, storage, and integrity of information
8. Reporting hierarchy, including elevation of issues to top management, legal advice, external experts, law enforcement, and regulators
9. Grading of levels of threats, consequences, and risks
10. Methods and order of procedures and options for addressing incidents, including options for prevention, response, mitigation, and remediation
11. Methods for exercises, drills, audits, and performance evaluation, including identifying performance metrics linked to the business objectives of the organization
12. Final report disposition, process review, and change management

While developing these procedures, the team leader should monitor if the threat assessment team has the appropriate breadth of competencies to be successful and determine what additional training might be required. The team leader should also determine if the makeup of the threat assessment team is appropriate to achieve its objectives and if changes or additions are necessary.

After defining its mandate and establishing its procedures of operation, the threat assessment team is now ready to begin its work defining the risk environment. The risk environment will be industry, organizational, and location specific. There is no one-size-fits-all approach. Defining the risk environment should include consideration of the following questions (many of which were discussed in the gap analysis to establish the program to prevent and manage violence in the organization):

- What are the strategic, tactical, operational, and reputational objectives of the organization?
- What are the functions and activities of the organization and how are its products and services delivered?
- What are the risks (likelihood and consequences) of violence related to these functions and activities (consider the different types of violence previously discussed in this book)?
- Who are the internal and external stakeholders who can impact or be impacted by a risk?
- What are the needs and expectations of internal and external stakeholders?
- What are the potential consequences on human, tangible, and intangible assets of a violent act?
- What current control measures are in place and what is their effectiveness?
- What programs of support, pre- and post-incident, that the organization offers to persons working on its behalf, are they well communicated and effective?
- What are the cultural, social, political, and economic factors that can impact the likelihood and consequences of violence? This should include access to and use of drugs, alcohol, and weapons.

Domestic, or intimate partner, violence is not confined to the privacy of an individual's household. These issues, and the associated stress, carry over into the workplace. Therefore, any assessment of the risk environment should consider intimate partner violence and how it is addressed within the organization. Does the organization provide support mechanisms for persons working on its behalf who might be in an intimate partner violence relationship?

When reviewing the risk environment, the threat assessment team should examine industry profiles for types of violence associated with their activities, workplace violence studies, accident and security incident reports, occupational health and safety reports, reports from the complaints and suggestion mechanisms, security and business continuity plans, local- and industry-based crime reports, audit reports, and external stakeholder complaints. In addition, reviewing business management documents, such as a SWOT report (strengths, weaknesses, opportunities, and threats) are helpful in understanding the context of the risk environment.

The threat assessment team will monitor the risk environment as well as investigate and evaluate reports of potential threats. There are both covert and overt behaviors exhibited by threat actors before an incident. When these behaviors are reported to the threat assessment team, it is their responsibility to launch an investigation to assess the threat. The depth of the investigation will depend on the intensity and veracity of the reported behavior or threat. The threat assessment team will also assess the immediacy of action needed. Investigations should always be fact based. Concerns reported by individuals in the organization are often based on that person's observation of a change in behavior in another individual or even another individual acting "odd." Once reported, a potential threat should be investigated and evaluated; however, care must be taken to avoid feelings and biases and dig for the facts. Focusing on facts will allow the threat assessment team to better judge whether intervention, counseling, elevation to law enforcement, or other actions are appropriate for the specific situation.

The threat assessment team may also identify potential victims of violence related to an activity or individual. Moving a potential victim from harm's way should be considered by the threat assessment team. Preventative and mitigation methods should be introduced as soon as practical.

It is helpful to conduct an initial assessment based on the report of a threat or behavioral issue. This is an assessment based on information in the report and immediately available (e.g. information from the human resources department, social media postings). The initial assessment should determine depth and urgency of a more thorough investigation, as well as the urgency of any immediate actions needed to protect potential targets of the threat. Both initial and in-depth investigations should answer who, what, when, where, why, and how. The in-depth investigation should also consider the root causes of potential violence. The simplest root cause analysis is asking the question "why?" five times for a particular set of circumstances. Understanding the root causes will help determine the appropriate prevention and mitigation strategy. Risk prevention and mitigation plans should contain indictors that trigger actions, the sequence of actions, performance indicators, and a review process.

The threat assessment team should be aware of its limitations. For example, understanding the workings of a person's mind is a challenge even for the most experienced psychology professional. Amateur psychological analysis can end up doing more harm than good. Seek external expertise when needed. Likewise, a risk assessment professional may be needed to conduct a formal in-depth risk assessment that will be used to develop preventative, protective security and continuity measures.

Considering and recommending appropriate actions and possible disciplinary measures should be based on the nature of the infraction, risk and threat assessment, and previous threat history. Actions may range from counseling, to reassignment, to temporary leave, to dismissal, to referral to law enforcement. The threat assessment team should set parameters for determining actions in an evaluation procedure and document the decision-making process. Everyone deserves a fair and equal vetting of the issues as well as a level playing field for actions administered regardless of rank or station in the organization.

INCIDENT RESPONSE TEAM

The incident response team will be tasked with initiating the immediate response to an incident to minimize harm to human, tangible, and intangible assets. It will also help de-escalate and stabilize the situation as much as possible.

It is important to always keep in mind that different people react to stress, both physically and mentally, in different manners. A person's ability to operate under stress may be very different from their abilities during normal conditions. It is prudent to screen the members of this team with a tabletop exercise to get an indication of how they operate under the stress of a violent incident. Members of the security management and/or business continuity teams often play a lead role in the incident response team. It is a good practice to coordinate the plans of the incident response team with security and business continuity plans.

The incident response team should receive training in alerting people within the organization that an incident is occurring, facilitate possible evacuation measures, provide first aid and triage for victims, and interface with first responders (law enforcement, fire, and medical teams) including providing ingress and egress information. The incident response team may also be tasked with coordinating the gathering sites after an incident and accounting for persons working on behalf of the organization that may have been impacted (and evacuated) during an incident.

The incident response team should also establish a routine to check the clearance of evacuation routes and the operational fitness of response equipment. This team may be tasked with conducting exercises and drills with the people working on behalf of the organization.

The incident response team should maintain the contacts list to use during an incident, obviously with a means to communicate. It is important to develop a relationship with first responders prior to a possible incident. A personal relationship helps to facilitate communications.

COMMUNICATIONS AND PUBLIC RELATIONS TEAM

The communications and public relations team is tasked with communicating with internal and external stakeholders. This includes families, the community, business partners, and the media. The communications and public relations team is responsible for developing the emergency communications plan. The communications plan should consider written, verbal, and electronic communications identifying people and organizations that should be proactively provided information. Develop communication templates for various risk scenarios in advance but keep in mind these situations are fluid and often need adjustments as events unfold. Communications should be internally and externally consistent using approved language, therefore, planned in advance. Given today's wide usage of social media, the team should have the competence to communication through appropriate social media methods.

The communications and public relations team should establish guidelines for designated spokespersons. Different people on the team may be assigned to interface with different groups (e.g. victims' families, business partners, media), but the message should be consistent. Designated spokespersons should be appointed. Note the plural, always have alternate spokespersons, a single designee might not be available during an incident. If the organization has a crisis communication plan, many of the communications procedures needed to address a violent incident are likely already described in a crisis communications plan for disruptive events (natural disasters, unintentional, and/or intentional disruptions)

The chief executive officer (CEO) of a company involved in the shooting incident was swarmed by media for details about the incident. Her response was "My number one priority is assuring the safety of all my employees. When I have more accurate information about the event, I will share it with you. Right now, my priority is my employees and their families. My colleague will provide you information about what we know for sure at this moment. Thank you." Control the message.

---

and can be applied to this situation. Crisis communications are frequently covered in business continuity and security plans, so these should be consulted.

The safety and security of all persons working on behalf of the organization and in the community should be communicated as the top priority during an incident. There is typically much confusion and uncertainty during an incident. Be honest and accurate, and avoid speculation and statements embellishing what you know to be facts. There is no harm in explaining that given the dynamic nature of the situation, more information will be provided as it can be verified. Using positive honest language, keeping the message short, and repeating key points help keep the message focused. Communicate what you feel you would be comfortable hearing in a crisis situation.

Information about victims should only be shared with their families or with family permission. Members of the communications and public relations team who are tasked with reaching out to family members and companions of victims should receive training in providing honest, sympathetic, and empathetic information. Also, they should be trained to communicate what counseling and assistance resources are available to address the stress and trauma of an incident.

RECOVERY TEAM

The recovery team is tasked with handling the aftermath of an incident including human assistance and operational recovery. Much of the work of this team may already be covered in the organization's business continuity plans. Furthermore, many steps involved in the recovery process are similar to recovery from natural disasters and accidents. Therefore, the team should consult with the business continuity officer in the organization.

One key factor in any recovery plan is learning from experiences to avoid a recurrence and improve performance. Therefore, the recovery team should collect data about the event in order to conduct a root cause analysis and identify opportunities for improvement. The objective is not to "return to normal" but rather to return to a "new normal" which strengthens the organization and avoids further incidents.

There are both mental and physical reactions to a violent event that may not be manifested immediately. Post-traumatic stress is not uncommon among victims and other people exposed to violent events. Assistance and counseling programs should be available to people working on behalf of the organization. Resources available to assist persons, working on behalf of the organization who have been impacted by a violent event, can be found in many communities from public sources. The recovery team should identify both private and public resources in advance of an incident.

The recovery process will involve implementing changes and improvements to the work environment. Change management needs to be well planned and paced at a rate that can be understood and absorbed by the people working on behalf of the organization. The change management program should consider the organizational culture and local culture to maximize success.

SYSTEMS AUDIT TEAM

The systems audit team reviews and evaluates the program to prevent and manage violence and identify opportunities for improvement. The audit team assesses if the program contains all the specified elements, how the elements interact with each other, and whether the elements are being effectively implemented. Other aspects of the program that the audit should assess include the following:

- Has the policy to prevent and manage violence been effectively communicated and implemented?
- Have the procedures to prevent and manage violence been clearly articulated and communicated to the people whom the procedures address?
- Are policies and procedures consistent with legal, regulatory, contractual, and other obligations?

- Are the issues identified in the risk assessment being effectively addressed?
- Is the procedure for risk and threat monitoring being effectively implemented?
- Are training and communications procedures adequate and effective?
- Is the system of managing violence being effectively implemented and integrated into the day-to-day activities of the organization?
- Are there opportunities for improvement?

The audits can be performed by persons internal and/or external to the organization. The auditors should be familiar with accepted internal auditing practices for management system standards. Audits should be evidence-based conducted by impartial and objective auditors. Therefore, ideally, the auditors should not be members of the other teams in order to avoid auditing their own work. At a minimum, auditors should not be responsible for the activities they are auditing.

An audit report should be prepared and provided to top management. This will allow for program review and improvement.

CROSSOVER MEMBERS AND LIAISONS

When teams operate as distinct units (rather than combined), they should not work in isolation. There should be crossover membership between the various teams, as well as team liaisons. Liaisons and crossover members need to focus on information flow between the various teams. Outside liaisons should also be developed with external stakeholders. Communication and information flow are two of the most essential elements of any management activity. In order to assure proper information sharing, it is best to have all the teams use a centralized recordkeeping system with clearly defined data access, confidentiality, and integrity procedures.

BUDDY SYSTEM

Creating a buddy system is a good practice to avoid people falling through the cracks. A buddy system involves pairing of individuals where the pairing assumes responsibility for one another's safety and welfare. It helps avoid isolation and estrangement. A buddy system can be implemented in businesses and educational institutions. Buddy systems are especially helpful in addressing the needs of individuals with special needs. Building a sense of belonging helps build a sense of "we are all in this together."

12

Risk and Threat Assessments

The risk assessment is arguably the most important decision-making tool at your disposal for planning how to prevent and manage violence in an organization. Risk is the uncertainty in achieving the strategic, tactical, operational, and reputation objectives of the organization. Uncertainty and risk can have both positive and negative outcomes, so when conducting the risk assessment, it is important to use it as a tool to identify and manage both threats and opportunities. Few, if any, organizations have unlimited resources yet most organizations face a wide range of risks they must address to achieve their objectives. Furthermore, most risks cannot be eliminated but must be managed. The risk assessment will provide a means to focus resources needed to manage a range of risks. Violence, which is associated with human behavior, is a risk category that cannot be eliminated and is rather variable in nature.

This section presents an overview of risk assessment and management concepts that can be used to manage violence-related risks in the organization. The concepts are the same as those that would be used to manage

---

Risk and threat assessments

As used in this book, "risk assessment" will refer to activities related to program planning and implementation. "Threat assessment" will refer to assessing threat levels during program implementation (e.g. assessing the threat of a specific threat actor or person of concern). The risk assessment is objective-based and looks at the big picture of preventing and managing violence-associated risks in the organization. A threat assessment is event-based and examines a specific scenario of a potential violent act.

---

any type of operational risk. It provides the basis for developing a comprehensive, consistent, and integrated approach to risk management to better understand specific risk issues and how they fit into the bigger picture of achieving the organization's overall objectives.

The risk management strategy should reflect a proactive approach that focuses on the achievement of the organization's objectives and what it is trying to achieve in terms of value creation (goods and services). This perspective of risk management differs from an older perspective that managing risk is about managing negative impacts of disruptive events. The objectives-based approach is akin to moving forward while looking out the front windscreen rather than a more reactive event-based perspective of driving while looking out the rearview mirror.

Given that your organization probably does not have unlimited resources to manage violence, the risk assessment will help prioritize risk treatments (measures to manage risk) needed to achieve organizational objectives. Therefore, it is important not to "silo" risks but to assess various risks simultaneously to determine how to best allocate resources. Also, many risk categories overlap, so conducting a comprehensive risk assessment can avoid duplication. Operational risks to consider simultaneously include those associated with intentional, unintentional, and naturally caused events (e.g. physical security, cyber security, natural disasters, crisis events, health, fire, safety, accidents, and harassment). Many of these operational risks will impact the objective of providing a safe and secure environment for persons working on the organization's behalf, as well as morale and productivity.

Most well-run organizations have an overall risk assessment and management approach. Start by examining the existing approach and determine how to best build on this. Having a standardized tool in the organization will make managing risk more seamless across divisions and activities. Two popular risk management models are based on the ISO31000:2018 Risk Management—Guidance standard (www.iso.org/iso-31000-risk-management.html) or the COSO Enterprise Risk Management—Integrated Framework (www.coso.org/Pages/erm-integratedframework.aspx). Both of these standards are objective-based and provide a generic framework for managing risks of all sorts. Does your organization currently have a risk assessment and management methodology? If yes, integrate your approach for preventing and managing violence into the existing model so that preventing and managing violence is considered a risk that needs to be considered in all day-to-day activities. If no formal methodology exists, see if the ISO31000 or COSO approach is more compatible with your organizational culture and way of thinking.

Regardless of the model used, it is important to always keep in mind that risk assessment and management is not an end in itself, it is the means to the end. Schools are in the business of educating children, so they have an objective of providing a welcoming, safe, and secure environment for learning. The risk assessment is a tool to elucidate how to achieve this objective by managing the uncertainties (including various forms of violence) that would prevent the achievement of this goal. Schools can be turned into fortresses, but how will this impact the allocation of scarce resources, and the physical and mental conditions conducive to education? Also, how does the fortress address issues that might be less spectacular, but exhibit higher prevalence, such as one-on-one violence, cyber bullying, verbal abuse, sexual and physical harassment, or suicide, which may exact a greater toll over a given period of time? What are the other issues (process improvements for safety or productivity, supplies, training, benefits and salaries, staffing, etc.) affected that are competing with security investments for funding? All these issues confront today's educators and businesses and need to be understood. The risk assessment will help prioritize risk levels and determine allocation of scarce resources.

RISK ASSESSMENT

The risk assessment should be conducted by the threat assessment team in conjunction with the persons tasked with conducting the risk assessment for the organization's overall management and other operational risks. Organizations operate in a dynamic, ever-changing environment; therefore, conducting a risk assessment is not a one-off activity, but rather an ongoing process. Risk assessments can be resource intense and time-consuming, so they should be carefully planned. Frequently, people associate risk assessments with looking for "what are we doing wrong." Avoid this perception by emphasizing that risk assessments are about identifying and opening doors of opportunity, not a "got ya" exercise.

It is very important to document a clear procedure for the risk assessment. Since you will be examining changes in the risk environment, it is very important that you have a consistent procedure to make comparisons of variables examined. Also, document the assumptions made and biases injected into the process. Everyone is a creature of their environment and experiences, so everyone has biases. Documenting biases may lessen their impact on outcomes. A thorough risk assessment will identify ways that you can make your organization more safe and secure. Risk assessments have the following common elements:

- Identification of the objectives, desired outcomes, and value proposition
- Definition of the internal, external, and risk management context (including characteristics and needs of stakeholders, supply/value chain, legal and contractual obligations, business and risk management framework, risk appetite and measurement)
- Risk identification (threat/opportunity analysis, vulnerability/capability analysis, criticality/impact analysis)
- Risk analysis (existing control measures, likelihood, consequences, risk levels)
- Risk evaluation
- Risk treatment
- Communication, consultation, and monitoring
- Documentation
- Review and improvement

It is important to consider all the elements. The order of using the elements may change based on how your thought processes work. It is a problem-solving exercise similar to solving a complex non-linear mathematical equation. There is more than one approach or algorithm that can be used to find a solution. Document the approach or algorithm (and associated assumptions) explaining the rationale behind the problem solving and the outcomes.

Assumptions that should be considered in any risk assessment are as follows:

- All risk of violence cannot be eliminated (this is actually more reality than assumption).
- Individuals (internal and external) have unique behaviors and thought processes, so they are always a dynamic variable in the equation.
- Time-based factors need to be considered.
- "It can't happen here" is an invalid premise. Believing that violence only happens due to bad people in bad areas is a bias that has been proven wrong over and over again.

RISK ASSESSMENT PROCESS ELEMENTS

Knowing your organization is an essential first step since it defines the reason for being. Why does your organization exist? What is its mission and objectives? Prevention and management of violence supports the achievement of those objectives. Consider different types and time frames of objectives. Strategic objectives relate to core business, strategy, goals and outcomes, and planning. Tactical objectives refer to midterm objectives related to achieving change: projects, mergers, acquisitions, and products. Operational objectives are related to routine activities.

Understand the value and criticality of your human, tangible, and intangible assets, as well as your activities and functions. These are what you use to create value and provide goods and services. This is also what you need to protect. Assess how critical each of the assets, activities, and functions are in achieving your objectives. What is changeable and how will changes impact your ability to provide goods and services? Consider people on the receiving end of your products and services (clients, customers, students, worshipers, etc.). They are also important assets to your organization because without them there is no business.

My guess is that almost everyone who has opened a school has the objective of educating people. I doubt that anyone has opened a school because they thought it would be an excellent means of investing their assets (people, time, and money) on security. A safe and secure environment supports the objective of educating people. Security measures are a means to support education objectives, not vice versa.

What are your internal and external stakeholders' needs and expectations? How do the stakeholders impact risk and how can they be impacted by risk? Understanding stakeholder traits is important and influenced by culture, religion, politics, social networks, and economics. The perception of risk varies from person to person and may not be aligned with actual risk, so you need to understand perceived risk and actual risk.

Identify the factors internal to your organization (internal context) that can impact your people, assets, activities, and functions. The internal factors include organizational culture, governance and management approach, structure and hierarchy, demographics, work ethic and morale,

101

resources, knowledge base, information systems and flows, change management approach, relationships, mission, goals, values, and access to weapons.

Identify factors external to your organization (external context) that can impact your people, assets, activities, and functions. The external factors include culture and demographics; interactions with external stakeholders (direct and indirect); attitudes toward violence; crime rates; access to and culture regarding weapons; legal and regulatory obligations; litigation climate; location and community influences; social, political, cultural, and economic influences; industry trends and competition; contracts and interdependencies; community resources; and perceptions and reputation. Legal and regulatory obligations and voluntary commitments vary by industry type and jurisdiction, as well as with time, so it is important to have a clear understanding of what are the specific obligations for your organization.

The internal and external context will define the risk environment. Risk environment changes from organization to organization and location to location (as well as with time); therefore, it is important to clearly understand the local factors that will impact risk. Understanding the risk environment and how it relates to your people, assets, activities, and functions is essential in determining a strategy to prevent and manage violence. Measures implemented to prevent and manage violence must be compatible with your organization's objectives and activities.

Define the criteria that will be used to define your risk assessment and management activities. How is risk currently managed in your organization and how does it integrate with the general business management approach? What is the organization's risk appetite (amount and types of risk the organization is willing to accept, pursue, or take in order to achieve its objectives)? One of the key criteria is to develop an agreed-upon system for grading risks, likelihoods, and consequences. High, medium, and low risk can mean very different things to different people. Therefore, it is very important to create a grading scale so that everyone is speaking the same language. To get risk within a range that is as low as is reasonably practical or acceptable, there is a need to define what the organization (as well as internal and external stakeholders) consider practical or acceptable. This also applies to assessing individual risks and threat levels. Predefine levels that can be used to both judge the seriousness of a threat (likelihood and consequences) and provide a basis for determining what actions will be taken. Not only does this support consistent analysis, but it also projects a sense of evenhandedness and fairness. It is not practical, nor is it good risk management practice, to try to eliminate or avoid all risks at any cost. There are no one-size-fits-all parameters for risk appetite. Since this is a subjective decision, it is very important to document the thought process, assumptions, parameters, and competing factors used to determine the risk appetite. Note that some organizations thrive and grow by setting a high risk appetite in order to pursue opportunities. They have made a management level decision to exploit risk for gain. In these situations, it is important that the risk appetite stay within the boundaries of an appropriate level of duty of care.

When assessing the impact of an act of violence materializing and determining the grading scales (severity) for risks, likelihoods, and consequences, it is important to consider the following questions:

- What are the physical and psychological harm and impacts to internal and external stakeholders?
- What are the direct and indirect impacts to families and other members of the community?
- What are the impacts on the supply chain and supply chain partners?
- What will be the financial impact in terms of human, equipment, and property losses and replacement?
- What is the potential for lawsuits and litigation?
- What is the potential for legal and regulatory fines and penalties?
- What is the cost in downtime, overtime, and lost productivity?
- What is the potential loss of revenues, sales, business, and customer base?
- What are the image and reputational costs, including negative press?
- If relevant, what is the potential stock devaluation and lost investment opportunities?
- If relevant, what is the magnitude of environmental impacts?

When considering the above questions, keep in mind that successfully controlling a negative event can become an opportunity. Therefore, to assess the value of different control measures ask, "What are the benefits if we get this right?" Investing more in controls to prevent an event can result in image and reputation enhancement, as well as increased morale and productivity and lower turnover rates.

Once the context is understood, it is possible to start risk identification. This includes a threat and opportunity analysis, vulnerability and capability analysis, and criticality and consequence analysis. Risk identification will illuminate what and how risk events contribute to uncertainty in achieving objectives. When conducting the risk identification, consider all the various types of violence that can impact the organization. This will help in understanding the priorities and relative impacts. It is virtually impossible to eliminate all the types of violence, so risk identification should provide the data needed to analyze relative risk levels and provide the information to prioritize risk and allocate resources to effectively treat risk. Risk identification should provide you with data of what can happen; who the potential threat actors are; and when, where, how, and why something could happen. Examine historic data, industry information, surveys and interviews with a range of stakeholders, discussions based on potential scenarios, and incident reports.

Assess existing risk controls and countermeasures. What formal and informal mechanisms exist that modify the risk levels? These can be awareness and training programs, administrative programs, policies and procedures, equipment and technology solutions, and cyber and physical security measures. How do these currently modify risk levels and what is their efficacy?

Analyzing risk involves evaluating the analyses from the risk identification step, combined with the analysis of existing risk controls, to determine levels of risk. The level of risk will be a function of the likelihood and consequence levels determined in the risk identification step minus the risk reductions due to existing control measures. Figure 12.1 illustrates how to combine the components of the risk identification step to calculate the level of risk. The risk analysis can be qualitative, quantitative, or a combination of both. The choice of method will depend on the purpose of the analysis, users of the analysis, and availability and reliability of information. As with any analysis involving living organisms, more complexity does not necessarily mean it is a better approach. Complexity should consider sensitivity and confidence levels as well as the needs to communicate the outcomes.

The level of risk is the input to risk evaluation. Risk evaluation will prioritize risk and guide the decisions for appropriate risk treatments (control measures). The risk level is compared to the risk appetite. If the risk level is higher than the risk appetite, it is necessary to evaluate a range of risk treatment options to bring the risk within the risk appetite. Risk treatment options can be single or multiple control measures. It can be a combination of human awareness, technical, engineering, administrative, operational, and/or protective measures. A cost–benefit analysis should be conducted for the various options which should include an analysis

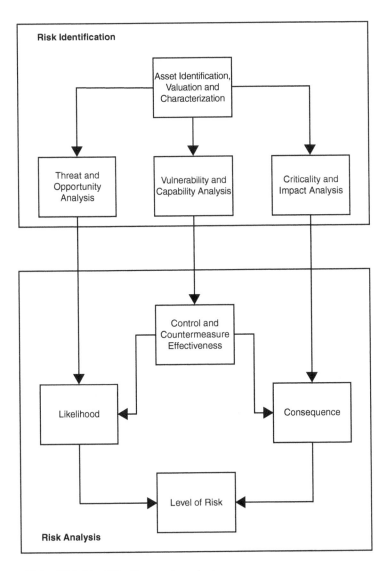

Figure 12.1 Risk identification and analysis.

of other risks competing for resources in the organization. Regardless of
the risk level being above or below the risk appetite, the risk evaluation
should also consider if there is a need for additional data and analysis,
if the risk appetite is appropriately set, and if there is consistency with

the organization's objectives. Since all risk cannot be eliminated, decisions made during the risk evaluation should be communicated and approved by top management.

Risk treatments should be a combination of adaptive, proactive, and reactive measures. Assume it is not possible to eliminate all risks, so consider the following alternatives, on their own or in combination with each other:

- Avoiding the risk
- Adapting internal or external parameters to change the nature of the risk
- Exploiting a risk to pursue an opportunity
- Eliminating or influencing the source of risk
- Modifying the likelihood
- Modifying the consequences
- Sharing the risk (e.g. insurance, contracts, outsourcing)
- Accepting the risk by informed decision

The choice of options that will be appropriate will depend on the type of violence that needs to be prevented and managed. Cost will also be an important factor in determining the right mix of treatment options. Regardless of the type of violence being addressed, protection of people should be the top priority. Therefore, a strong focus should be on managing the human element through awareness, training, and screening programs. Remember, you are protecting humans from other humans, so management and behavior control methods need to complement technology and physical security measures.

The risk assessment and organizational objectives should directly advise the awareness and training programs, screening and vetting protocols, and determination of appropriate physical and cyber security measures.

> Weapons do not kill—they are inanimate objects. People with weapons kill. People with more powerful weapons kill more people.

Preventive and preparedness measures should be the top priority whenever practical, but humans are a very variable species, so it will be impossible to prevent all acts of violence, particularly when faced with a motivated, resilient, and innovative threat actor. Therefore, response, contingency, and recovery planning are also needed. These plans are also advised by the outcome of the risk assessment and consideration of achieving the organization's objectives.

THREAT ASSESSMENT PROCESS

A threat assessment is event based and examines a specific scenario of a potential violent act. Threat assessment will be carried out by the threat assessment team for both threats related to activities and functions in the organization, as well as to analyze reports of specific incidents, threat actors, and individuals of concern. It may be necessary to complement the threat assessment team with outside expertise experienced in conducting risk and threat assessments. When seeking outside expertise, care must be taken to select advisors who understand the organization and its objectives, as well as the local risk environment.

Threats of different magnitude, severity, and urgency will be reported that will warrant further investigation. Do not just dismiss a threat report. Any threat reported should be followed up with an assessment. It is best to conduct the investigation as a multistep process. Threats determined to have low magnitude, severity, and urgency can be closed out quickly if data indicate low risk. However, threats with medium and high magnitude, severity, and urgency will require a more in-depth threat analysis.

Depending on your communication mechanisms, a threat will be reported by either internal or external stakeholders to the team leader of the threat assessment team and/or a designated person in the human resources department. It is best to have a subgroup of the threat assessment team conduct the initial review of a threat report.

A synagogue in the United States hired an Israeli security consultancy to develop its violence prevention and emergency management plan. They assumed the Israelis had more experience dealing with violent events. The management plan considered attacks and threat actors that have been part of the Israeli experience but did not consider the local context. The primary focus of the management plan and risk treatment was based on a scenario of a politically/religiously motivated suicide bomber wearing an explosive belt attacking the synagogue. Not addressed were workplace violence, active shooter events, hate crimes, graffiti and vandalism, estranged spouse abductions of children in daycare, or natural disasters. All these issues are more common and likely in the local context.

This group will determine if there is sufficient information to launch an investigation. If there is not sufficient information and data, then this subgroup should identify information-gathering needs and seek additional information. If there is sufficient information to launch an investigation, the subgroup needs to make a preliminary judgment about magnitude, severity, and urgency. In the initial assessment of the threat, consider the following:

- What is the credibility of the threat and the information provided (e.g. is it physically possible)?
- What is the potential for damage and harm to people and assets?
- What are the jurisdictional laws and regulations as well as liability issues involved?
- What are the implications of ignoring or downplaying the issue, especially if it materializes?
- How will this impact organizational performance and reputation?
- What is the scope of the threat and the scope of a threat assessment and control measures?

Low-likelihood and low-consequence issues associated with low magnitude, severity, and urgency may not require the entire threat assessment team for resolution. Based on the threat assessment discussions of the team leader and subgroup members, a determination of actions necessary to mitigate and remediate the situation should be launched. The persons involved in the report should be consulted during the discussions to make sure they feel their concerns have been addressed. A closeout report should be prepared by the team leader, as well as determining what monitoring steps are needed.

At the other end of the spectrum, issues with high likelihood and high consequences with accompanying high magnitude, severity, and urgency should trigger immediate action. This may also require bringing in more expertise and law enforcement personnel. The threat assessment team should immediately launch an in-depth threat assessment and investigation along with mitigation and remediation measures. The in-depth threat assessment should determine who, what, where, when, why, and how related to an incident and persons of concern. Corrective measures should be launched to stabilize the situation. Once the situation is stable, the threat assessment team can discuss root causes and potential preventative measures that can be implemented to prevent a recurrence.

Situations that are deemed high/medium likelihood and low/medium consequences or low/medium likelihood and high/medium consequences accompanied by varied or uncertain magnitude, severity, and urgency

Many grading scales exist. Scales can use terms such as insignificant, low, medium, high, extreme, or numerical scales 1–3, 1–5, and 1–6. The number of gradations in the scales may vary in number and if the total number of grades is an odd or even number. The best choice is based on the thinking processes of the graders; more is not necessarily better. The key factor for success is to clearly define the boundaries and parameters for each grading level so that all the graders are using the same units of measurement.

should trigger further assessment and investigation of the threat and of persons of concern. Similarly, incidents that cannot fit into one of these three classifications should also trigger further assessment of the threat and investigation by the entire threat assessment team. The team leader should first review the threat assessment team for the appropriate mix of competence and views to assess the threat. Is there the right mix of experts (e.g. experienced threat assessors, human resources, psychology experts or counselors, legal and liability, process owners, safety, security, law enforcement, labor or family representatives)? Is there sufficient information and data available to conduct the assessment and investigation, if not, what data needs to be gathered? What immediate measures can be taken to de-escalate the situation?

For all the above classifications, the team leader in conjunction with the threat assessment team, human resources, and legal counsel should define a clear and consistent procedure for conducting the threat assessment and investigation. Similar to the risk assessment, it is very important to define the grading scales and parameters (criteria) for the boundaries of the classifications. Define what is meant by low, medium and high. What are the boundaries for determining magnitude, severity, and urgency? One size does not fit all, so these parameters need to be defined by each organization. They will be dependent on factors such as risk appetite, the level of burden of proof, liability concerns, culture, sense of time, and types of consequences (human, financial, reputation/image, operational, environmental, and indirect costs).

The risk assessment and investigation procedures should include a performance evaluation of the assessment and investigation, procedures for privacy and information security and integrity, communication and reporting protocols, and ongoing monitoring. The procedures should be regularly reviewed for effectiveness and to identify opportunities for improvement.

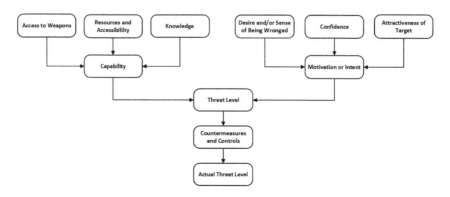

Figure 12.2   Determining threat levels.

Analyzing threats made by threat actors needs to consider that the level of threat will be based on the capabilities and motivation/intent of the threat actor. Therefore, it is helpful to break down the components of capabilities and motivation/intent when conducting the threat assessment as illustrated in Figure 12.2.

For each scenario, threat actor, or person of concern, the threat assessment team should investigate and discuss all the components that comprise capability and motivation/intent. Never assume "it can't happen here" or other forms of denial. When assessing the components, consider the following:

- Physical and cyber access to a target
- Vulnerabilities of the target
- Physical and competence capabilities of the threat actor
- Access, ability, and knowledge of weapon usage (including types of weapons)
- Access to information needed to plan an attack (e.g. insider and/ or outsider intelligence gathering)
- Attitudes toward violence as a means of conflict resolution
- Sense of being wronged
- Social, political, economic, racial hatred, religious intolerance, and cultural motivators
- Attitudes toward revenge and justification in the culture
- Desire for martyrdom, suicide, escape, or notoriety
- Ability the threat actor to acquire the means to conduct an attack
- Threat actor's sense of achieving objectives

- Threat actor's relationship with a target and perception of what can be gained
- Resilience and determination of the threat actor
- Potential sympathizers, allies, apologist, and collaborators

Determine how the existing countermeasures and controls will modify the likelihood and consequences of an act of violence. Things to consider that modify likelihood and consequences to determine the actual threat levels include the following:

- Physical security measures to prevent, detect, deter, delay, deflect, and respond to an incident
- Cyber security measures
- Alarms and notification systems
- Emergency management procedures (including evacuation plans)
- Awareness and training programs
- Policies and procedures
- Administrative protocols

Given the ubiquitous use of social media in today's society, it is important to analyze online and off-line presence of a person of concern. Risk and threat assessments, and investigations, should focus on evidence and facts, not just how people feel. Therefore, information and data should be collected from various sources (e.g. document review, previous incident reports, interviews, physical evidence, observation of activities). The team leader should develop a threat assessment and investigation plan and review the plan with the entire threat assessment team from the outset. The threat assessment team must decide how much information needs to be gathered to reach a credible and fair conclusion. When developing the plan, the threat assessment team should also consider what impact the threat assessment and investigation will have on the organization and its activities, as well as the people involved. Poorly conducted investigations that negatively impact people can result in a decrease in the flow of intelligence.

The outcomes of the threat assessment and investigation should be reviewed by the group of people tasked with deciding the appropriate actions and corrective and preventative measures to take. Not only should the threat actors and person of concern be considered but also how to prevent a recurrence and how to address identified vulnerabilities. Consider every threat assessment and investigation an opportunity to improve day-to-day operations.

From the discussion above it is clear that risk and threat assessments can be very complex. For novices, it may be best to solicit the assistance with someone experienced in conducting the assessments. An external set of eyes may also help you see things that you overlook because they have become routine or mundane. Having a neutral party question your assumptions often adds a very valuable perspective to a discussion.

13

Indicators and Information

Preventing and managing violence in organizations involves under-standing and predicting human behavior. Understanding the behavior of humans has been an area of intense study since scientific research began. Variability and complexity is enormous, and most "predictive" indicators work best in hindsight. Most traits that are used for predictive indicators can be attributed to large portions of the population. For example, expo-sure to violent movies and games is a trait shared by many individuals who have committed acts of violence. However, only a very small percent-age of people who enjoy violent movies and games ever become some-one who perpetuates a violent act. Bias also influences how we interpret human behavior. Everyone has biases that have accumulated from their life experiences and what they are familiar with. Most people are more comfortable with things they are familiar with and more afraid of things they are not familiar with, they do not identify with, or are unknown. Therefore, extreme care must be taken when interpreting predictive indi-cators. The threat assessment team needs to recognize and document its biases and make every effort to conduct their work in an organized, consistent, and structured way to minimize bias and perform their work using an evidence-based approach.

It should also be recognized that some decisions will need to be made based on incomplete information. This may be due to an urgent need to respond to a potential threat and/or inaccessibility and unavailability of information. It is important to collect as much information as practical using a structured evidence-based approach, documenting any gaps in information or knowledge. An assessment should be made of the accuracy of the information and the reliability of the sources of information. An assessment should also be done to determine if any bias has been injected into the data collection exercise. For example, availability bias is seeking information and examples of things that are more recognizable or retrievable than representative. Likelihood can be exaggerated by overweighing the frequency of an event because information about that type of event is more available or the event itself more easily recalled.

The analysis of indicators and information is a complex exercise that is difficult for inexperienced threat assessment teams. Therefore, until the team has sufficient competence to conduct assessments on its own, it is highly recommended to seek assistance from an experienced threat assessment professional. This is a unique expertise that many chief security officers and physical security practitioners do not possess, so it is best to seek someone with this specialization and/or a background in psychology and human behavior analysis rather than just security experience.

When assembling the threat assessment team, it is very important to include a broad cross section of persons with different roles in the organization and perspectives. Team competence not only includes a balance of knowledge and background but also perspectives to try to minimize bias and groupthink. Indicators and information can be interpreted in different ways and is often influenced by a person's past experiences; therefore, discussion of information with people from different backgrounds can highlight points that might be missed by a more homogeneous group.

BIAS AND ASSUMPTIONS

Bias and assumptions are natural in many problem-solving exercises. This is particularly true of analyzing human behavior. Therefore, it is important to identify and document any biases or assumptions. Various forms of cognitive bias exist, including, but not limited to, the following:

- Stereotyping
- Denial and "it can't happen here" bias
- Social, cultural, and gender biases
- Familiarity and confirmation bias
- Perception, observational selection, and memory biases
- Belief and behavioral biases
- Relational, groupthink, and tribal biases
- Confirmation biases
- Information availability and recall bias

- Hindsight and post-rationalization bias
- Decision-making biases
- Illusion of control biases
- Time perception biases
- Courtesy, self-validation, and acceptance bias

The above partial list of biases illustrates those that may exist in members of a threat assessment team. During the discussion and documentation of biases, the team leader should determine if any members of the threat assessment team are too entrenched in their biases to conduct an evidence-based investigation. These persons may adversely impact the investigation, and the team leader needs to determine if they should be excused from a particular investigation.

Complex problem solving and decision making based on incomplete information involves making simplifying assumptions. Assumptions should be documented and their impact understood. Questions to consider to determine the validity and impact of assumptions include the following:

- What are the assumptions based on? Opinions? Evidence?
- Do the assumptions reflect a bias?
- Do the assumptions eliminate factors and information thereby oversimplifying the problem?
- Do the underlying assumptions impact the outcomes?
- What is the impact of the level of uncertainty on the assumption?
- How do the assumptions affect the confidence in the interpretation of evidence?
- Would a different person make different assumptions?
- Would the outcomes be different if they were based on different assumptions?

During threat and risk assessment processes, revisit the assumptions. Were the assumptions made still valid in light of the evidence and data gathered? It is also a good idea to revisit the assumptions and biases at the end of the investigation to determine if the conclusions are an artifact of the assumptions or evidence based.

Another consideration is determining the validity and reliability of the information that is being used in the threat assessment and investigation. When reviewing the information, you are considering how do you know something rather than what do you think. Some questions to consider include the following:

- What are your sources of information?
- How reliable are your sources of information?
- What are the biases or agendas of your sources of information?
- How consistent is the information you received?
- Are there corroborating sources?
- What is the context of the information?
- Are there alternative sources of information and what are they indicating?
- How did you verify the information?
- Do you understand the information and is it complete?

INDICATORS AND INFLUENCING FACTORS

Human behavior is very complex, and the answer to why some people resort to violence and others, given the same stimulus, do not is an open question and an ongoing field of psychological study. After every incident, there is an effort to understand "why." In hindsight, it is often possible to determine an individual's path to violence, but it is often difficult to understand why a certain person committed the act of violence when others who travel a similar path do not become violent. Therefore, care is needed in using the indicators of potential violent behavior. In the discussion below, the author typically uses the following assumptions:

1. "It can't happen here" or "he/she is not the type" are not valid arguments. Persons of interest and threat actors come in all sizes and shapes, as well as all economic classes, races, religions, genders, educational background, and walks of life. Therefore, assume anyone could potentially be a person of concern or threat actor.
2. Making a threat and posing a threat may or may not be linked. Not all violent acts are predicated by a threat, and not all threats are followed by an act of violence.
3. A complete picture is needed in an evidence-based investigation to determine levels of concern and actions that need to be taken. A single indicator is not sufficient to make a conclusion. Rather, it is necessary to examine both the pattern of multiple traits, behaviors, factors, and conditions, as well as changes in these patterns to conduct a thorough analysis. In mathematical terms, this is

a problem of solving a nonlinear partial differential equation (sounds complicated, it is).

4. The characteristics of the person of concern, the target, and the risk environment need to be considered. Understanding the internal and external context of the risk environment is essential for assessment and management of violence.

5. Based on the type of violence, the level of spontaneity varies. Seldom do people just snap, many if not most forms of violence involve some planning and forethought. Therefore, evidence of patterns and changing behaviors, planning, and preparation need to be monitored and reported.

6. Fairness, consistency, and a focus on facts rather than emotions are critical to an investigation.

7. It is not possible to predict future events with certainty, and the past does not always foretell the future. Copycat events do take place, but every investigation should be conducted on the specific facts and evidence of the case being analyzed.

8. Threat environments are volatile and subject to change. The organization and people working on its behalf need to be resilient. Likewise, many threat actors and persons of concern are resilient. Threat actors have the capability to change their plans and actions when observing the defenses.

9. There is a correlation between committing a violent act and suicidal tendencies, a desire to kill or be killed, and domestic or intimate partner violence. These factors should be considered keeping in mind the variability inherent in the correlation.

10. People are your most precious asset and your best line of defense. Prevention, training, and awareness programs should emphasize a preemptive and proactive perspective.

11. Err on the side of protecting your people, tangible, and intangible assets.

12. Societal and personal coping mechanisms will play a role in determining if a threat actor turns into a violent person. It is necessary to not just look at indicators but also to consider coping mechanisms and attitudes in the individual, organization, and community.

13. Access to weapons and attitudes toward the use of weapons (personal and societal) will play a role in the potential for violence.

14. It is better to be overcautious and wrong than to be in denial and wrong.

15. You will never be right 100% of the time. Therefore, all incidents are also learning experiences to learn from mistakes and factors missed.

This list of assumptions illustrates the difficulty of the task the threat assessment team is facing. Therefore, it is really important to have a defined standard operating procedure for conducting the activities of the threat assessment team.

A sense of injustice, unfair treatment, or being wronged can manifest itself in any of the types of violence. This may lead to a perceived need for settling scores, a quest for justice and righting a wrong, and a justification for revenge. Therefore, the sense of injustice, unfair treatment, or being wronged should be monitored as an indicator of potential violence, and information should be gathered to better understand the root causes of this feeling. For example, a sense of economic and social disparity may drive criminal activity (robbery, assault, terrorism) common to Type I violence as well as establish a justification in an individual and community that while criminal activity might be wrong, it is understandable in the quest for justice. Likewise, in Type II violence, both impulsive and planned violence may occur by people who feel that they have been wronged or aggrieved by interactions that do not meet their expectations.

A history and sense of abuse, bullying, ostracism, and harassment (physical and mental, online and off-line, real or imagined) are indicators of potential issues. Depending on an individual's coping mechanisms and support from the community, the time frame for planning and taking action, as well as the form of act, can vary significantly. The threat assessment team needs to carefully consider the urgency and type of response needed when this indicator is present.

Changes in behavior and life situations are indicators and information that needs consideration. Part of risk awareness training should emphasize that these are warning signs that should be reported to the threat assessment team when linked to a perceived higher level of risk or a threat. Examples of these behaviors and indicators include, but are not limited to, the following:

- Life changing experiences and evidence of serious stress (death, divorce, job loss, financial problems, illness)
- Diminished functional capacity (physical and mental)
- Changes in medication and substance use (e.g. stopping or increasing the use of medications, substance abuse)
- Changes in performance and lose of interest in performance

- Communicating intent for violence and/or fascination with violence (oral, written, and in social media)
- Increased abuse and harassment of others (physical or verbal, online or off-line)
- Threatening, stalking, or other intimidating behaviors
- Detachment from possessions, depression, social isolationism, or suicidal tendencies
- Sense of isolation, hopelessness, nothing to lose, or inability to fit in
- History of domestic or intimate partner abuse or violence (physical and mental)
- Unhealthy or degenerating social, family, work, or community support systems
- Extreme social, political, or religious beliefs coupled with growing intolerance of others
- Obsessive behaviors, expressions, and actions toward other persons
- Expressing the need to seek revenge for perceived religious, political, social, or economic wrongs
- Narcissistic, sociopathic, or psychopathic behaviors (particularly changes in behaviors)
- Unexplained or new extreme, impulsive, or erratic behaviors
- Expression of anger and poor anger management
- Complaints of being wronged, persecuted, victimized, or treated unfairly by others
- Desire for recognition or notoriety
- Deliberate human and animal cruelty or property damage
- Sense of others not meeting expectations and frustration with activities in the organization
- Making plans for end of life and giving away possessions (unexplained making order)
- Mood and personality changes (e.g. a sudden sense of calm or increased agitation)

These behaviors do not have a cause and effect for violence. In fact, many people can exhibit many of these traits and never become violent. Also, the weighting and influence of these traits will be different in different people. However, people who do resort to violence typically do exhibit some or many of these traits, so these can be used as indicators both for awareness and reporting procedures, as well as factors to examine during the threat assessment team's investigation.

After each spectacular mass killing, the media is filled with terms describing the assailant as "mentally ill," "weirdo," "odd," "socially awkward," "extremely introverted," "extremely extraverted," or "loner." This is usually accompanied by an interview with someone who knew the assailant who claims: "I always knew this would happen someday." It may be possible in hindsight to trace the path to violence that might include these traits, but most people with these traits will never commit a violent act against another person, much less a mass killing.

When looking at the above list, it is also clear that an individual's coping mechanisms coupled with family and community support mechanisms can dampen the effects of many of the traits. Therefore, programs that provide counseling or a social safety net (e.g. family, friends, and community support and intervention) can mitigate the risk. In the workplace, conflict resolution and mediation counseling can help de-escalate tensions. Activities that give purpose to life (e.g. relationships, a cause to pursue, social and religious belonging, or different work, tasks or hobbies that provide a sense of accomplishment) can help mitigate a potential for violence. Unfortunately, all too often individuals can only be helped if they have access to assistance programs and are amenable to the program's de-escalation and assistance activities.

In addition to monitoring behaviors, there are also some indicators that are signs that a violent action may be in the planning stage. Is a person of concern making threats? Is a person of concern surveilling a target or facility? Is a person seeking information and conducting unexplained questioning that might be used in an attack? Are there unexplained purchases of materials that could be used as a weapon or weaponized? Are comments being made that justify or praise the use of force as a means of justice or revenge? Are acts of violence (real and from entertainment) being glorified or praised as legitimate conflict resolution methods? Are materials being positioned and physical facilities being changed (e.g. access controls or escape route changed) that might make an attack possible? Is the person of concern damaging inanimate objects or harming animals? These questions are often indicators that something is already in the planning stage. If the answer is affirmative to any of these questions, fellow workers, parents, friends, and teachers should err on the side of caution and notify the threat assessment team or appropriate health services and law enforcement resources in the community.

INFORMATION COLLECTION AND ANALYSIS

Assessments and investigations should be based on facts and data. Therefore, the threat assessment team needs to identify appropriate information sources and determine their reliability. There is not always the luxury in terms of time, resources, and availability to pursue all the data and information desired for evidence. The team should consult with legal counsel to determine if there are privacy or other jurisdictional laws and regulations that may restrict access to certain types of information. Sources of information may include the following:

- Background screening, work history, and performance evaluations
- Family history including records of any domestic abuse or intimate partner violence (physical and mental)
- Social and electronic media postings and/or information on electronic devices
- Employment and personnel records
- Educational records and performance evaluations
- Criminal records
- Public service and military records
- Substance abuse and drug use history
- Health records (physical and mental)
- Crime statistics
- Financial and economic information
- Entertainment choices and club memberships

The information can be gathered in interviews, physical examination, or observations. The Internet allows access to a variety of open-source information, social media, and blogs. These should be considered in monitoring and investigation procedures.

DOMESTIC OR INTIMATE PARTNER VIOLENCE AS AN INDICATOR

Signs of an abusive relationship may not be obvious. Abuse may be mental or physical, perpetrated and received by any gender, race, religion, or social or economic group. Understand the limitations (ethical and legal) of your organization to intervene in domestic or intimate partner violence to determine what actions are possible. Given that domestic or intimate partner violence is a risk factor that can spill over into the organization, consider the following signs of a potential problem:

- Signs of anxiety, stress, fear, distress, depression, or suicidal thoughts
- Signs of physical abuse especially if accompanied by implausible excuses
- Change in ability to conduct activities and declining performance (lack of focus or caring, inconsistency in quality of work)
- Disruptive visits to the organization by the possible abuser (especially if accompanied by threats or weapons)
- Evidence of stalking and other unwanted contact by abuser
- Absenteeism or chronic lateness or reluctance to leave work
- Overly or unexplained concern about the whereabouts of abuser
- Desire of the abused person to hide their whereabouts
- Unexplained requests for time off to handle a crisis at home, counseling, or court appearances
- Unexplained requests for changes of routines or schedule
- Abnormal number of communications which elicit a strong emotional response or fear to use communication devices
- Inappropriate or offensive physical or electronic communications particularly of an insulting, degrading, or threatening nature
- Mood swings, sudden temper, anger, overreaction to criticism, withdrawal, or sense of isolation
- Inappropriate clothing or overly heavy makeup to hide injuries
- Unexplained fear of job loss or financial stress or access to money

Monitoring these behaviors may be an indication that someone is a potential victim, or an indication that someone may evolve into a person of concern. Will domestic or intimate partner violence spill over from home into the organization? Monitoring indicators and encouraging participating in assistance programs can help prevent escalation of the problem.

ACCESS TO WEAPONS AS AN INDICATOR

It is fairly safe to estimate that 100% of people who committed a violent act with a gun had access to a gun. Most weapons were from within their own household. While access to weapons is an indicator for the potential for violence, it must be recognized that only a small percentage of gun owners become assailants. However, there is a solid correlation between being shot by a gun and a gun being present. Some organizations feel that access to a weapon is a powerful enough indicator that they ban any weapons from their properties or facilities. Access to weapons and attitudes toward the use of weapons are risk factors that cannot be dismissed.

After a recent incident of targeted violence with a gun, employees of a company in a risk awareness meeting discussed how to lower the risk of gun violence in their workplace. Access to weapons, particularly firearms, was considered a significant risk factor that should be used as an indicator. The conclusion of the discussion was that in addition to a complete ban on weapons in the workplace, it would be helpful to identify all gun owners for additional training and monitoring. The job application was modified so that during the application process gun owners would have to identify themselves and list the weapons they had access to. Providing misinformation on the job application was already terms for dismissal. During orientation, persons working on behalf of the organization were told that weapons purchases needed to be reported to the human resources group. Gun owners were required to take weapons safety training and implement the measures to securely store and transport their weapons. People who were identified as having access to weapons who then were reported to the threat assessment team were given expedited screening and investigations. To date, no incidents have occurred, so the effectiveness of the approach has not been determined, but it was determined that morale and an enhanced sense of safety was felt in the workforce.

PUTTING INDICATORS INTO PERSPECTIVE

Dr. Linda Zangwill, Professor of Ophthalmology at University of California, San Diego Medical School, suggests the following medical analogy to appreciate the sensitivity of individual indicators. A reality check on the use of indicators is to consider their positive predictive value. In standard medical terminology, this term is used to determine how likely it is for a patient with a positive test result to have a specific disease. Translated into predicting acts of violence, how likely is it that a person with a certain characteristic will commit an act of violence? The positive predictive value depends on the prevalence of the disease, or in this case, acts of violence. The prevalence is the total number of acts of violence divided by the total population (number of people). The positive predictive value of any individual indicator is the number of actual violent persons divided by the total number of people predicted to have the indicator trait. The positive predictive value of the ability of individual indicators to predict future violent acts is very low. The low positive predictive value suggests that many of the individual indicators are weak predictors of future violent acts. Looking for patterns of multiple predictors or changes of behavior related to the predictors may improve their predictive accuracy.

14

Communications

One of the most essential elements of a program to prevent and manage violence in an organization is robust mechanisms for communications. Communication plays an important role before, during, and after an event. Communication mechanisms need to enhance the flow of information both inside and outside the organization. To be effective, communication needs to be a two-way street where people feel their voice is valued.

Risk and security awareness is based on effective communications. The human resource department should work with the threat assessment team and communications team to develop communication plans and establish mechanisms for communications. All persons working on behalf of the organization should receive orientation and ongoing training in the available communication mechanisms.

Communications should be tailored to the audience. Within an organization, this may require

"If You See Something, Say Something"

The United States Department of Homeland Security has an initiative called: "If You See Something, Say Something" (www.dhs.gov/see-something-say-something/what-suspicious-activity). Many other countries have similar initiatives. The underlying concept is that suspicious behaviors (not appearances) should be reported. This concept should be integrated into programs to prevent and manage violence in organizations. To accomplish this, it is important to have robust communication mechanisms to enable both internal and external stakeholders to communicate with the organization and the threat assessment team.

segmenting the communication approach for specific groups. Not all groups within an organization need the same information. Also, when deciding on a communications approach, it is a good practice not to overwhelm people with too much information at one time and to target only relevant information that they can use. Language used in communications should also be tailored to the language and education level of the receiving audience. Also, in today's multicultural, multilingual society, it is important to consider special language needs, as well as persons with special needs.

Communications mechanisms need to be established with first responders (law enforcement, fire, and medical). Clear lines and mechanism of communication with first responders need to be planned and implemented as a proactive measure. With whom and how is first contact made during an incident? What information will they need in order to effectively respond to an incident? What do they need to know about floor plans, ingress, and egress? The best way to find out is to invite them to your organization and ask how you can work together. Keep in mind that first responders learn from each event they respond to and improve their techniques. Therefore, communication is an ongoing process, not a one-off activity.

When designing the communication mechanisms, first examine the existing systems in the organization. Can you leverage existing system capabilities to meet the needs of the program for preventing and managing risk of violence in the organization? Start by looking at what has been created for security, business continuity, and emergency management plans. Addressing violence in the organization will include elements from security, business continuity, and emergency management plans, so for consistency build on and improve existing mechanisms. Also, consider "dual-use" applications and mechanisms. The objective of any organization is creating value, goods, and services. Your communication mechanisms can also help increase productive and morale in the organization, so consider how to integrate with day-to-day business management practices. To maximize the effectiveness of any communication plan, the following building blocks are recommended:

- Have a clearly defined and written policy, process, and procedure.
- Assess user needs (including special needs groups).
- Consult with legal counsel to meet privacy, legal, and regulatory requirements.
- Determine what information needs to be shared with whom.
- Consider capacity requirements during normal operations and during an incident.

- Consider compatibility and consistency with other communication processes.
- Determine the type of communication mediums that are appropriate and effective for each audience.
- Develop awareness and training on communication mechanisms for persons working on behalf of the organization.
- Determine testing and maintenance requirements.
- Establish information flow protocols. This should include two-way communications to respond to messages received.
- Establish recordkeeping and information security protocols.
- Identify performance indicators.
- Review performance and effectiveness.
- Implement improvements as needed.

When developing the communication mechanism consider both internal and external stakeholders that need to be kept in the loop. Consider that people under stress often are not functioning, physically or mentally, as they would under normal, less stressful situations. Your ability to communicate during an incident will impact your reputation and image. You may only get one chance to make the right impression, so proactive planning of communications is essential.

When developing a communication plan, things to consider include the following:

- Who are the target audiences and what are their needs?
- What are the appropriate modes of communication—how will you contact internal and external stakeholders?
- What are the contact numbers and emails for family members, first responders, medical assistance, psychological assistance, law enforcement, support programs, and others that may need to be contacted if an incident occurs or can be prevented? Who should have this contact information?
- How will you alert people in case of an incident?
- How will you communicate during an incident, including what communication networks are available during an event and what is their capacity?
- Are phone or message trees effective in communicating with various stakeholders?
- How do you communicate with people with special needs and disabilities?

- During an incident, how do you need to communicate to keep track of all persons working on behalf of the organization?
- During an incident, communication may cause a risk. For example, how do people safely communicate without divulging their location to a threat actor? Can a threat actor, or media, exploit access to the communication system? Can access to non-controlled communications create misinformation and fear?

RISK COMMUNICATIONS

Identify both internal and external stakeholders who can impact, and may be impacted by, a violent incident in your organization. Do not forget to consider business partners, neighbors, and the larger community. How will you warn people in the case of an incident? Can alarms and alerts developed for accidents and natural disasters be leveraged, or do they potentially have conflicts with alerting people about an act of violence? Are panic buttons an option? How will first responders be alerted and what information do they need? When answering these questions, consider both how and what information can be shared?

Both internal and external stakeholders need and want to know how the organization prevents, responds to, and manages violence. If the organization wants to send a message that managing violence is everybody's responsibility, this requires empowerment of the workforce, which requires two-way communication and the sharing of information. Your workforce may be your most important source of intelligence. If they understand what, why, when, and how to communicate, then there is a greater chance of receiving timely intelligence. If they sense that they are just being talked to and are not privy to information they feel they need as risk managers, it is quite likely that they might not be as engaged in sharing information.

Consider this example. The chief security officer had been a combat marine, and then served in the local police SWAT team until he retired and became a chief security officer for the organization. His approach was telling people in the organization what he was doing to make them safer and telling them what he felt they needed to do. He was not shy in pointing out that as an ex-combat marine and SWAT officer, he understood violence. He did not see the need to explain or consult with others in the organization because "what do they know about security." The approach did not give the workforce a sense of security and productivity suffered. Top management decided to merge the security functions with the other operational risk management activities. The risk manager (in order to better educate herself about the situation) initiated "town hall" meetings with different groups in the organization from maintenance crew to management. She kicked off the conversation by asking each group to consider their day-to-day activities and explain to her what they felt were potential threats to successfully carrying out their activities. Were there potential things that might happen that would disrupt their activities? Not surprisingly, the people "in the trenches" who were considered to be uninformed by the chief security officer offered up valuable information on how they could do their job better. The maintenance workers (in many cases, innocently and at first, hesitantly) offered up actionable information about not only their specific activities but also things they observed around the organization. The risk manager decided to recognize the people who spoke up in the company newsletter. She also decided to conduct "town hall meetings" monthly and add a recognition system and small rewards for actionable information. Everyone now felt that their voice was valued, and they were part of a team. Both morale and productivity increased in the organization. Use of the suggestion box message system increased. Moreover, now that people understood how they fit into the bigger picture of the organization, the town hall meeting discussions and suggestion box evolved beyond just security issues to include suggestions for work safety and process improvements. Yes, there were some suggestions of little value, but the organization discovered that recognizing people who were willing to share concerns and identify problems, greatly improved the comfort level of sharing information and enhanced morale.

There are many choices for methods of communication (audial, visual, written, and electronic). What is the appropriate method for the demographic of the group being communicated with? Will passive communication methods work, or will the message be lost in the background noise of other communications? What are the technology usage requirements and constraints for sending and receiving information? When is it too much and people begin to tune out? Will false positives and false negatives result in people no longer listening? What is the boundary between sounding an alarm and being an alarmist?

NOTIFICATION, COMPLAINTS, GRIEVANCES, SUGGESTIONS, AND WHISTLEBLOWER MECHANISMS

Notification, complaints, grievance, suggestions, and whistleblower mechanisms are good practices not only for preventing and managing violence in the organization but also for day-to-day business management. People who feel that their voices can be heard and their input is valued typically feel more inclusion as well as a sense of ownership of the activities they engage in. However, having an integrated mechanism will only work if it has a defined process to get the information to the appropriate parties without delay. If this objective of expeditious delivery of the information cannot be assured, it may be better to consider a specific system tailored to prevent and manage risk.

Establish and publish a policy for complaints, grievance, suggestions, and whistleblower mechanisms clearly stating that input from all persons working on behalf of the organization is encouraged and that anyone who files a complaint, grievance, or suggestion will be safe from retaliation. The policy should state that complaints, grievance, suggestions, and whistleblower mechanisms are intended to resolve issues, enable accountability for actions, and seek improvements in operations to better prevent and manage violence. The policy should also reflect a commitment from the threat assessment team, human resources department, and top management to expeditiously investigate all complaints respecting the rights and dignity of all persons involved. The policy should also state a commitment to due process, fairness, confidentiality, and timely resolution. The policy should articulate how external stakeholders (companions, friends, family, customers, and other affected persons) can submit their concerns for investigation.

To support prompt and equitable resolution of complaints, grievances, or suggestions, the organization should establish and publish (to internal and external stakeholders) the complaints, grievance, suggestions, and whistleblower procedures. Procedures should explain the following:

- The submission process—both anonymous and non-anonymous methods using written, oral, and electronic means can provide multiple paths of submission. Different people will feel more comfortable using different approaches, so give a choice of submission methods.
- Explain what information is required from the submitter to initiate an investigation. Who, what, where, when, why, and how are the minimum questions to answer. Include a means to submit corroborating evidence.
- Encourage submitters to explain "why" there is a threat or concern if possible. Addressing why helps conduct a root-cause analysis, which can identify corrective and preventative actions.

- Define roles, accountabilities, and time frames for the complaint to be investigated.
- Explain the hierarchical and procedural steps involved in the investigation and resolution process.
- Describe potential punitive, remediation, and corrective measures that may be taken and how they will be equitably applied;
- Describe what will be the form of output of the investigation and with whom this information will be shared.
- Explain information handling protocols including how information will be accessed (and by whom), confidentiality, security storage of information, and maintenance requirements.
- Describe how information shared will be used to drive continual improvement and how investigation findings will be used to take action to remediate (including a description of options for disciplinary actions) and prevent a recurrence.
- Describe under what circumstances the investigation will be expanded to include outside authorities.
- Explain how investigation outcomes will be documented and communicated to the parties concerned. Reinforce the process for privacy and confidentiality.

The gunman was very meticulous in planning his attack. As an employee, he was very familiar with fire drill procedures and the company's designated escape routes. He began to place obstructions and locks on escape routes days ahead of his planned attack. The nighttime cleaning crew thought this was odd, but simply assumed this was something planned by others in the organization. The organization had failed to communicate an effective suggestion and complaint mechanism, emphasizing that everyone's input is welcome.

Once the policy and procedures have been developed consider how to communicate the process to both internal and external stakeholders. It is important to include external stakeholders, for example, parents and other family members, as well as friends, often are aware of warning signs of potential violence. Alerting them that communicating concerns and the non-retaliatory nature of the process may encourage the reporting of important intelligence. Emphasize the positive—that the process is to provide support for persons working on behalf of the organization and improve security and safety in the organization.

131

Also, explain that persons submitting a complaint, grievance, or suggestion will be protected from retaliation, unless it is clear that a submission was fraudulent and intended to cause another person harm or embarrassment.

All complaints, grievances, or suggestions should be regularly reviewed by the threat assessment team to identify any patterns that might raise concerns. The review should also assess the performance of the complaints, grievance, suggestions, and whistleblower mechanisms to identify potential improvements.

SUPPORT MECHANISMS

It is important to communicate and promote the use of employee assistance and other support mechanisms. Persons working on behalf of the organization should be aware and feel comfortable accessing these services. When promoting these programs, emphasize that this is for the good of the individual and the organization. Explain confidentiality and privacy measures to protect individuals. Also, explain that accessing these services does not harm an individual's standing within the organization.

PERFORMANCE REVIEWS

Honest and regular performance reviews are helpful to communicate to individuals where they stand with regard to their job performance and explain any concerns. Some acts of violence can be traced to individuals feeling they are not being treated fairly and being "shocked" by criticism of their performance. Face-to-face performance reviews may give an opportunity to observe behaviors that may become problematic.

EMERGENCY GATHERING POINTS AND FAMILY REUNIFICATION AREAS

The organization needs to designate emergency gathering points and family reunification areas before an incident takes place. This information needs to be effectively communicated to appropriate internal and external stakeholders. The effectiveness of these procedures should be tested when conducting exercises, since they will likely play a role in most response actions. Gathering points and reunification areas should be complemented by another mode of communications (e.g. texting, phone or web based) to account for individuals after an incident. The reality is that some people will feel they are running for their lives and will leave the area. Unless they are accounted for, precious time may be lost searching for people who are actually clear of the event. When communicating the family reunification areas, it is worthwhile to explain to family members that the incident is best handled by trained professionals, and their interference may actually hamper response times.

15

Exercises and Drills

One of the most important tools an organization can use to prevent and manage violence is to have regular exercises and drills. Exercises and drills help create a culture of security and risk awareness. They reinforce the importance of personal responsibility and the need for individuals to take action to protect themselves and their coworkers. Testing plans helps identify potential weaknesses and illuminate opportunities for process improvements. Exercises and drill are also useful in screening the response teams for their ability to handle stress. Also, repeated practice helps build muscle memory to enable people to respond more efficiently, thereby reducing response times.

Simulating a scenario helps increase awareness but care must be taken to monitor and manage stress levels during an exercise. Practicing to prevent and respond to a violent incident will likely increase the stress levels in many people. Therefore, exercises need to be objective, process, and demographic appropriate. Exercises and drills need to be designed for their learning and awareness outcomes. By testing existing measures and refining new methods and procedures, exercises can build team dynamics and better collaboration among different role players in a planned response. However, keep in mind actual events seldom follow your plans, so design in flexibility to impart competence to response to actual situations.

Exercises and testing should also be conducted to test specific procedures and technology solutions that have been implemented. Does the procedure or technology have the capacity to operate as expected during actual situations? For example, will the communication systems (technology and procedures) have sufficient capacity to continue to operate as planned during a crisis? Are ingress and egress routes accessible, clear of obstacles, and sufficient to enable access to responders? What are realistic time frames for responses of internal and external stakeholders? Have people been adequately training to implement the procedures and technologies to manage an incident?

Two major techniques for surviving an attack are shelter-in-place/ hide or evacuate/run. Exercises and drills should practice these skills, which are also important in dealing with natural disasters, fires, and accidents. Start by examining existing procedures for fire and safety plans. Can the procedures and exercises developed for fire and safety plans be leveraged for the prevention and management of violence. Are their aspects of fire and safety plans that may not be appropriate for acts of violence? Conducting an exercise can help identity what can be leveraged and what needs to be changed.

Exercises and drills are advised by the risk assessment and treatment outcomes. The risk assessment will shine light on the likelihood and consequences of an act of violence, as well as the types of violence that may impact the organization. Therefore, the scenarios are drawn from the risk assessment. This will also help assess the validity of risk assessment assumptions and conclusions.

The team planning an exercise should draw from members of the threat assessment team, response team, and human resources, as well as include health and safety officer, chief security officer, and other emergency response personnel. The planning team also needs to contain representatives from the units undertaking the exercise. This latter group is especially important to point out potential risks to people and processes in their units that might be due to the exercise. Roles should be designated in the team. The team leader or facilitator develops the scenario, controls the flow of the exercise, and manages the exercise. A controller introduces the injects (problems to solve) into the exercise at the instruction of the team leader. Observers observe and document the actions of participants in the exercise.

To be effective, exercises and drills need to be carefully planned and executed. All exercises and drills should have a "kill switch," a clear predefined signal that the exercise or drill needs to be immediately halted for the well-being of the people involved. It is a good practice to invite first responders to also participate in exercises and drills, not only does this have the benefit of getting to know each other for better coordination, but many first responders have experience conducting drills and exercise and can provide invaluable insights. Exercises are a careful balancing act of executing scenarios that are realistic and able to prepare people for a real situation, managing stress levels created by exercises, and maximizing learning potential of the exercise. Storylines (scenarios) need to be carefully thought out to achieve the exercise objectives while not scaring and intimidating people. This is particularly important in exercises and drills in educational settings where exercises and drills need to be age appropriate and not invoke fear in children. If kids fear their schools as dangerous places because they have been traumatized by an exercise or drill, then it defeats the major objective of educational institutions: educating children. Start simple when planning exercises. As the exercise program becomes more mature, it is possible to increase the complexity of the exercises.

EXERCISE METHODS

There are several exercise methods. The general categories below are listed in terms of increasing complexity, time for planning and execution, and stress levels:

1. Conversation-based exercises—These are excellent learning tools for developing, implementing, and assessing the performance of policies, plans, and procedures. They include lectures, seminars, and workshops. As with many lectures, seminars, and workshops, audience participation and dialogue improve learning outcomes.

2. Tabletop and limited simulation exercises—These provide a narrative storyline (scenario) where participants discuss their roles in the defined situation in a non-threatening environment. Participants review and discuss the actions they will take in the situation. A facilitator can monitor stress levels and manage the tabletop by steering the pace and

A medical device company conducted regular exercises. They felt stress levels increased too much and learning outcomes were not meeting expectations. The risk manager decided to try making the exercises entertaining as a means to lower stress levels. Conversation-based exercises were converted to interactive online cartoons. Tabletop and functional exercises tested response to invasions of zombies, vampires, or Martians. Learning and retention rates improved.

direction of the exercise. These exercises are excellent tools for clarifying and practicing roles and responsibilities, as well as identifying opportunities to improve policies, plans, and procedures. They are also useful in identifying how an individual might operate under stress.

3. Functional exercises—These are exercises that are operations based. A storyline (scenario) is conducted in a realistic environment where people can walk through their roles in the actual setting. This provides a real-time assessment of the efficacy of procedures and equipment. It provides the ability to evaluate human, technology, and equipment capabilities. Typically, emphasis is placed on testing policies, plans, procedures with the intended users. These are excellent for testing command and control structures along with communication plans. Functional exercises will be more effective if they include internal stakeholders along with external stakeholders (e.g. first responders). Since these are real-time and realistic, there will be a need for more extensive planning to address higher stress levels. They are a good mechanism for determining who in your organization can continue to operate effectively under stress.

4. Full-scale exercises—These are the most complex, stressful, and resource-intense exercises. Careful planning is essential and extensive. Understanding risks related to the exercise is crucial. Full-scale exercises are for testing a realistic and real-time scenario with both internal and external stakeholders in the actual environment. In other words, they are simulating a real incident with both internal and external players. The intent is to mirror a real situation as much as possible, so assume that internal and external stakeholders can be potentially negatively impacted by the stress and fear of the real-life scenario. Also consider that people participating in the exercise might respond as if it was a real event—what does that mean for the people playing the role as threat actors?

SIMPLE PLAN-DO-CHECK-ACT APPROACH

There are many approaches to designing and implementing an exercise or drill. Figure 15.1 illustrates a simple plan-do-check-act (PDCA) approach. The approach can be used to both evaluate plans to prevent

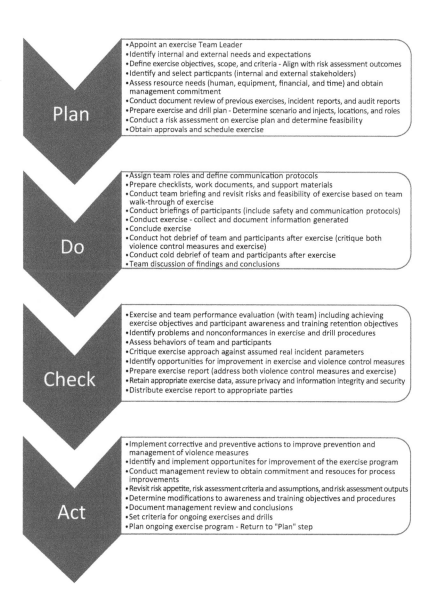

Figure 15.1 Exercise and drill process.

and manage violence as well as to review and improve the exercise program. Note that the PDCA approach is actually a continual improvement cycle. Figure 15.1 is drawn as a flow diagram for legibility.

139

16

Incident Prevention and Management

Incident prevention and management measures should address avoidance, prevention, preparedness for, response to, and recovery from violent events. Avoidance and prevention measures ideally are the top priorities; however, no matter how thorough, it is not possible to eliminate all risks. Therefore, procedures need to consider the best combination of controls and countermeasures that will minimize the risks and their consequences before, during, and after an event.

Implementing security measures in isolation is a partial solution. For security measures to be effective, it is necessary to understand why they are being implemented and how they will benefit the objectives and value-added proposition of the organization. People are more likely to comply with security procedures if they understand the reasons for the procedures. It is also insufficient to just tell someone, "this is your security obligation." It is essential that they understand how and why they implement the measures to achieve the security objectives. Security measures also need to be understood and applied at all levels of the organization and by all relevant stakeholders, including external stakeholders who can impact or be impacted by risks associated with violence in the organization. Essentially, to be successful, security measures need to impart a sense of ownership among the affected stakeholders.

Consider a threat notification system. It is possible to develop a mechanism and procedures to channel threat information for analysis and investigation. Unless the mechanism and procedures are explained to the target users in terms of why, how, what, where, and when they have a responsibility to take action, it is likely that the mechanism and procedure will not meet its potential as a risk control measure.

From the perspective of the threat assessment team, security officer, and human resource personnel, awareness of the reasons for the risk controls and countermeasures should highlight how they are providing a valuable service to the organization and the achievement of its objectives. Performance indicators should emphasize how their efforts to prevent and manage violence help to achieve the mission and objectives of the organization.

Top management often views risk controls and countermeasures (particularly for low-likelihood security and continuity events) as an organizational expense with unclear return on investment. Fear tactics are sometimes used and may provide a short-term stimulus to action, but for sustainable benefits, performance indicators based on parameters such as enhanced morale and sense of security, improved productivity, lower turnover and absentee rates, organizational loyalty, and improved work atmosphere will likely have more long-term benefits. Linking risk, security, and continuity measures to value creation performance metrics will have a greater chance of sustained management support and program funding.

When developing risk controls and countermeasures, it is important to include the owners of the activities and processes in the organization. These include management from all levels, engineers and line supervisors, and representatives of people conducting the actual activities. If controls and countermeasures conflict with the performance objectives and tasks of persons working on behalf of the organization, they will not be considered as appropriate by those who need to use the procedures. After every mass shooting at a school, a chorus of security solution-providers try to market an array of security technologies and equipment, playing on the fears from the recent events. Many of these solutions (some very costly) have not demonstrated that they would make a difference in actual field conditions. While many will indeed harden a target for a similar type of attack, they must be considered within the context of the purpose and objective of an educational institution. Does the solution increase fear or contribute to an environment conducive to learning? What are resource trade-offs and maintenance costs? What are the manpower, awareness, and training parameters and costs to make the solution effective? What are the life cycle costs? Does the security solution create other risks (e.g. information technology vulnerability, privacy violations)? Do the measures conflict with good fire safety measures and protection from natural disasters (e.g. tornados, earthquakes)?

It is a widely accepted practice in safety and security management that a layered approach to controls and countermeasures is the most effective. If one layer of protection or type of defense is breached, another will hopefully provide the necessary control. A threat actor needs to penetrate the vulnerabilities of all the layers to successfully attack a target. For each layer introduced, determine how the control measure will change the likelihood and consequences of an incident and if the risk has been lowered to an acceptable level. It is also good practice to layer measures that prevent, respond to, and help recover from an incident. When considering what is the appropriate number and types of layers, some considerations include how to

- Promote risk and situational awareness.
- Avoid and prevent an incident.
- Preposition resources to contain, stabilize, and manage an event.
- Respond to mitigate the impact of an event and protect lives.
- Respond to minimize damage to the organization and its value chain.
- Recover to a new normal.

A comprehensive plan will hopefully avoid or prevent an incident. Since that is not always possible, the plan then considers how to de-escalate a situation to minimize harm to people and manage the degradation of activities and functions to stabilize and continue operations. The plan also recognizes what are the critical functions and activities and in what order and time frame they need to be restored. The plan also needs to consider the aftermath of an event to learn from the experience and restore operations to a new normal.

When developing violence prevention and management plans, it is important to be aware of legal, regulatory, contractual, and liability issues. With regard to prevention and management of violence, duty of care would dictate that doing nothing is not an option. Even if many violent events may be considered low-likelihood events, many are high-consequence events, therefore some form of treatment and contingency planning is necessary to demonstrate an appropriate level of duty of care.

Any program to prevent and manage violence in organizations should consider how to incorporate these essential areas into planning:

- Management commitment
- Inclusion—top-up and bottom-down participation
- Awareness and training emphasizing personal responsibility and actions

- Tailoring to realities at each site and community
- Phased approach paced to the absorptive capacity of the users
- Setting realistic and maintainable goals
- Recognition and feedback loops

AWARENESS AND TRAINING

Awareness is an ongoing activity that fosters a culture of alertness of actions that can impact safety and security. It requires a top-down, bottom-up approach, where all persons recognize that their actions impact and can be impacted by risks. Risk awareness programs help people recognize threats; report issues to appropriate authorities; and respond to protect human, tangible, and intangible assets. Awareness sensitizes people to security and promotes an inclusive culture where everyone sees preventing and managing the risk of violence as a mutual benefit and an integral part to achieving objectives.

Central to fostering an awareness culture is recognizing that organizations and individuals need to take ownership of their risk environments. When organizations and individuals take responsibility for the risks that impact them, and which, in turn, they impact, they act as a force multiplier. Therefore, both internal and external stakeholders need to be aware of the programs and procedures available to prevent and manage violence. For example, parents need to be aware of the reporting and support mechanisms available at their children's school to seek help if they detect unusual and potentially volatile behavior in their children. Parents need to be educated to identify indicators in their children of violence to themselves and others, as well as what are the reporting and support mechanisms and how to use them. Mechanisms should also provide the opportunity to report issues such as harassment and bullying that may lead to more violent acts.

Surveillance cameras monitored by a security officer may not be as powerful as empowering people to be aware of their surroundings and reporting potential issues. Furthermore, responding to rapidly evolving events, such as terrorist attacks and active shooter incidents, requires people to assess and respond to the incident to protect themselves and those around them. Equipment and technology can help, but investments in training and awareness significantly improves the chances of safety and survival.

An awareness-training program is an effective means of embedding risk and security thinking into an organization, as well as heightening the awareness of community members. Key to an effective program is targeting the delivery of relevant information tailored to the appropriate audience in a timely and efficient manner. This should be supplemented with clearly defined ongoing communication channels. The program should be developed and driven in collaboration with the threat assessment team and human resources staff to effectively target new hires, reclassifications, and general staff. To enhance the retention of information and emphasize the importance to the organization, it is best to repeat the same information multiple times using different media and communication methods.

Management commitment is another element essential for success. Managers at all levels need to reinforce to the people they supervise that managing risk is a core value of the organization. They need to promote risk and situational awareness as an integral part of day-to-day activities. Managers need to encourage their personnel to recognize and report threats to achieving the organization's objectives, as well as protect human, tangible, and intangible assets. Obviously, this includes building appropriate reporting mechanisms and protocols, as well as responding to threat reports in a formal and timely manner. When building a reporting mechanism, it is critical that all persons working for the organization understand that highlighting concerns is not a sign of paranoia, disrespect, or betrayal, but a means for the organization to operate more effectively and prevent issues that may escalate into violence.

Recognition and reward schemes for employees who report concerns help drive the cultural change for people to speak up and be involved. For example, the Pathfinder Group in Pakistan has a very robust program for risk awareness training, communicating concerns about changes in the risk environment, and suggestions for improvement in operations. Employees are recognized and rewarded for suggestions that make clients and employees safer and/or that improve operations and services. All standard operating procedures for activities in the organization include a description of internal and external stakeholders who could impact or be impacted by the procedure. The standard operating procedures also describe potential risks that could affect the execution of the procedure, as well as risks associated with the procedure. Training on procedures, even for mundane activities, includes a discussion of risks. Performance evaluations consider the role of employees in managing the risks associated with their activities. This has helped create a family atmosphere in the organization (which has thousands of employees) where employees feel their well-being is a top priority. It has also created a steady flow of intelligence that has helped the organization address issues that could have potentially escalated into undesirable events. Pathfinder has found that between the awareness and recognition program and their benefits package (including health care), they have reduced their turnover rates to levels that are the envy of their industry, and this in turn has significantly reduced recruitment, screening, and training costs, not to mention led to a significant increase in customer satisfaction ratings.

Security awareness programs may also be used to drive a general awareness of organizational goals, further empowering people to understand and promote the organization's objectives, making the organization more resilient. Therefore, the awareness program should provide training related to understanding the following:

- The roles and responsibilities related to achieving the organization's objectives.
- How the individual's role in the organization impacts risks and can be impacted by risk.
- The organization's violence prevention and management policy, procedures, and practices.
- The administrative, managerial, operational, tactical, and technical controls to protect human, tangible, and intangible assets.
- A clearly articulated non-retaliation policy for persons who report verbal and physical behavior which they reasonably believe represents a threat of potential violence.

Awareness is not just within the domain of organizations. Family and members of the community need to work together to promote awareness and create channels of communication. Too often, three- and four-word slogan campaigns substitute for awareness programs. Slogan campaigns too often rely on fear to identify and respond to "suspicious behavior." Without accompanying training, this may potentially increase the risk of unfair and unjust targeting of individuals with different skin color, religious symbols, language, or cultural practices. To avoid biases, people need to understand what constitutes "suspicious" activity and behaviors, otherwise people may simply report behaviors that make them uncomfortable because they vary from the perceived norm or conversely discourage people from making reports due to fears of being accused of prejudice or concerns for being wrong. Slogans are helpful for getting the overall message across, but it is the accompanying training that results in informed reporting and fewer false positives.

146

In any awareness and training program, the ultimate objective is to instill a sense of ownership in the risk management process. In many cases, this may require a cultural change within the organization. Cultural change cannot be forced; rather, it needs to be paced at a rate that can be absorbed by the stakeholders. It needs to demonstrate the value added by the changes along the path of the change process. Cultural change needs to be carefully managed and have the participation, support, and commitment from top to bottom and bottom to top.

Successful cultural change is accompanied by an attitude change. After working in security on several continents, and in risk environments ranging from the Middle East and Central Asian to Japan, one thing has stood out as a key differentiator. The differentiator is a sense of "we're in this together" and ownership. People taking responsibility for security and people looking out for each other in their family, organization, and community appears to be the key ingredient for success. Ironically, even in high-risk environments, it has been my experience that people who take ownership and responsibility for security in the activities and functions they conduct seem to have a greater sense of security and safety than in lower risk environments where security is seen as the responsibility solely of a chief security officer, law enforcement, or the government. Equipment and technology play an important role in prevention and protection. Adding additional weapons to the mix is very debatable. Time and again, I have seen nurses, maintenance crews, cleaning staff, groundskeepers, line workers, process engineers, and safety and environmental managers identify risks and recommend workable solutions to manage the risks. In almost all cases, I have seen this accompanied by a more positive attitude and morale in the workforce. Conversely, I have seen cases where managing risk is considered the responsibility of someone else where the same groups of people skirt security procedures and protocols because they do not understand their role and responsibility. I have seen this accompanied by a greater sense of fear and uncertainty. Ownership and responsibility seems to instill an enhanced sense of control of one's destiny. Again, I qualify this paragraph by stating that this is a generalization based on my experience in working with organizations in different countries and in different risk environments. It has led me to conclude that preventing and managing violence in an organization must be seen as a human resource and business management issue as much as it is considered a security issue.

INCIDENT PREVENTION AND MANAGEMENT PLANNING

One of the key responsibilities of the threat assessment team is to develop a strategy to prevent and manage violence. This should be a team effort in order to leverage group perspectives and knowledge. The team determines what are the types of violence (I—VI) that the organization is exposed to and the frequency of each type of event based on crime statistics. The team needs to recognize that just because statistics for your type of organization and activities are low does not mean it will not happen. Start by collecting some primary data to start the analysis. For each of the types of violence, the threat assessment team needs to rank if your organization is considered low, medium, or high. Start with the following questions:

- What are the functions and activities in your organization that are exposed to each of the types of violence?
- How would an incident impact the organization's objectives and human, tangible, and intangible assets?
- Who are the stakeholders (internal and external) who can be impacted or impact each of the types of violence?
- What are the characteristics of the work environment (physical and people related) that may affect the likelihood and consequences of an event and can they be manipulated?
- How does the type (e.g. main facility, field services) and hours (e.g. time of day, season) of services provided affect the levels of risk?
- How might an event manifest itself?
- What would be the likelihood and consequences of an event occurring (low, medium, high)?

Be careful with statistics. Different numbers may provide different impressions. Absolute numbers will give the number of events, but was the information gathered using similar methods, or have numbers changed because of changing reporting and monitoring methods? Relative numbers can be deceiving. A high rate of change may be due to absolute numbers being very small, so each additional event is seen as a very large rate of change. What are the numbers actually measuring? Has the number of incidents actually increased, or has the power of the weapons used increased to escalate the damage done? What are the numbers actually telling you? One hundred percent of active shooter events in the United States have been caused by someone from a gun-owning household, predominately by a white male. So?

148

- How do these rankings change from location to location based on the local risk environment?
- What are the types of controls and countermeasures currently in place and do they focus on before, during, or after an event?
- How do the current controls and countermeasures reduce the likelihood and consequences of an event?

The data collected is used to initiate a structured brainstorming process among team members. There are many methods that can be used depending on the makeup of the team and cultural group thought processes. Worksheets, flow diagrams, and "mind mapping" help keep the discussion focused. Figure 16.1 is an illustration of a relatively simple mind mapping approach derived from the approach introduced in the 1960s by Dr. Kaoru Ishikawa, a quality control expert at the Faculty of Engineering at the University of Tokyo. This figure will help identify the types of risk the organization needs to consider, along with the internal and external context and influencing factors to consider. This provides input into the analysis of events, controls, and consequences. The visual depiction of information helps focus the discussion and also communicate the outcomes.

Figure 16.1 illustrates a range of risks that the organization faces, beyond just preventing and managing violence. While this significantly complicates the discussion, it does have several advantages:

1. Several participants on the team may not have any background in security but can identify issues not previously considered violence-related issues by thinking about what might impair the achievement of objectives in their activities and functions. Likewise, security experts

Mind-mapping is a brainstorming technique that diagrams the relationships of elements comprising a problem or system. Its origin is attributed to ancient Greek philosophers and has been adapted as a tool in assessing risk. Integrated into the organization's system of management, it provides a useful tool to both analyze and communicate uncertainties in achieving the organization's objectives. Various techniques (e.g. threat tree, fishbone, Ishikawa, and bow-tie diagrams), standards, and software packages use the mind-mapping concept. It can be used as a method of analysis as well as a decision-making tool for choosing controls and countermeasures. The threat assessment team can use a mind mapping approach to leverage experience and knowledge of team members.

149

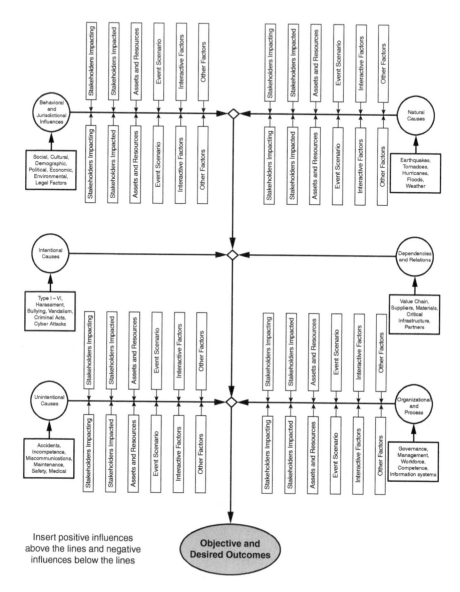

Figure 16.1 Risk diagram for uncertainty in achieving objectives.

might not be aware of the administrative, procedural, and process nuances associated with many functions and activities.

2. It highlights positive factors that influence and contribute to the achievement of objectives. This helps build a sense of ownership and participation and ingrains the cultural concept that security is an integral part of all aspects of the organization's activities. It will help identify performance metrics and other factors needed to promote awareness in the organization.
3. It helps identify the root causes of events rather than just focus on reactive mechanisms. This provides information to address causes used in avoidance and preventative measures rather than just addressing the symptom of the causes.
4. It highlights trade-offs and resource issues (priorities and limitations) that need to be presented to top management decision makers in order to receive the necessary management and resource commitment for a successful prevention and management program.
5. It teases out various stakeholder needs and requirements that need to be addressed while highlighting the business management indicators that can be used to demonstrate the value-added proposition of the program. Remember, regardless if it is security, safety, or environmental protection, measuring nothing happening for low-likelihood events (especially if they have never occurred) makes it very difficult to sustain commitment and investment with competing resource priorities.

Now that there is a clear understanding of the big picture, it is possible to laser focus on the main risks of concern in the program, risks associated with Types I–VI violence. Turn to a deep dive discussion of intentionally caused events emphasizing Types I–VI. For each type of violence, have a discussion of different event scenarios, their likelihood, and consequences (include both tangible and intangible consequences) and identify the current controls and countermeasures. Also, identify what is the risk appetite and what would be considered what is as low as reasonably acceptable or practical (risk reduction target). This is depicted in Figure 16.2.

The output from this step serves as the input for the next step—analyzing the risk levels and determining what combination of controls and countermeasures is the most appropriate to bring the risk within an acceptable level of tolerance. The next step uses a "bow-tie" diagram, which gets its name from being shaped similar to a bow tie. Its origin is unclear, but I have heard many Australian risk managers claim that it

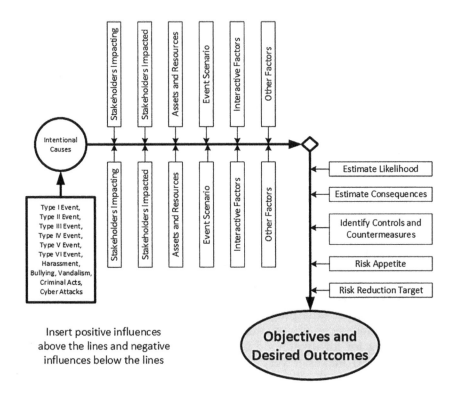

Figure 16.2 Risk diagram for uncertainty in achieving objectives due to intentional causes.

has its origins in Australia to complement the Australian-claimed "Swiss cheese" model of layers of protection.

The bow-tie diagram, illustrated in Figure 16.3, is a very useful visual tool for analyzing the causes and effects of an event that may alter the achievement of an objective, outcome, or activity. Keep in mind that a bow-tie diagram focuses on one type of event at a time. On the "Prevention and Preparedness" side of the diagram, the different threats, or event causes, are listed that may lead to an event following the path labeled "event mechanism." On the "Response and Recovery" side of the diagram, the possible effects or consequences of the event are listed following the path labeled "consequence mechanism." The vertical boxes represent layers of controls and countermeasures that change the level of risk. Escalating factors look at factors that may cause a control measure not to operate as planned and

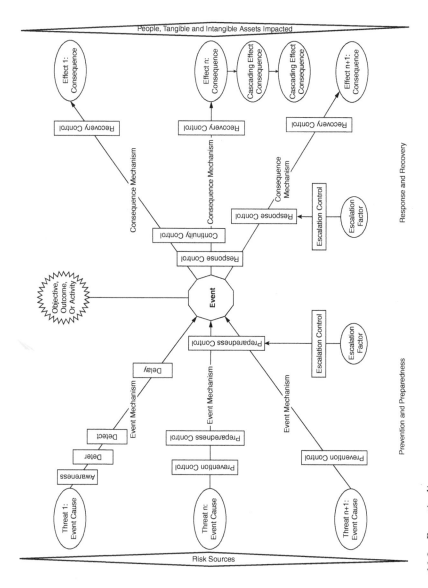

Figure 16.3 Bow tie diagram.

examine the incorporation of escalation factor controls. When using the diagram, consider the "interactive factors" identified in Figures 16.1 and 16.2 to understand the interactions between various causes and effects, as well as consider the potential for cascading consequences. In addition to layering controls and countermeasures, Figure 16.3 illustrates that efficiencies are achieved by control measures that change the risk levels of multiple causes or effects. It is helpful to note frequency and severity estimates for event causes and consequences, as well as steps along the path of the mechanisms to indicate risk levels before and after control measures.

A rough bow-tie diagram can be used during the team discussions to identify and analyze risks. A subset of the team can summarize the discussions in clean bow-tie diagrams for a revisit by the team to make sure assumptions are valid, biases are understood, and diagrams are complete. The diagrams are now ready to present to top management for decision making about the appropriate control measures and necessary allocation of resources.

Using the Swiss cheese model as depicted in Figure 16.4 (thank you Australia!), consider what the appropriate blend of layers is. There may or may not be cost-effective techniques for each potential event for each type of violence. Per amount of resources invested, what gives the greatest return in terms of percentage of risk level decreased? Experiment with combinations of risk reduction and mitigation techniques to reach a level, within the risk appetite, that is as low as reasonably allowable or practical. Unless you have

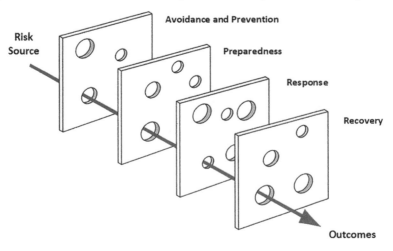

Figure 16.4   General Swiss cheese diagram.

access to unlimited resources, or you choose to ignore other risk issues that may have similar or greater impact, a point will likely be reached where:

- Costs and trade-offs, or shortchanging more likely risks with higher impacts are prohibitive.
- Expenditures become disproportionate to additional benefits.
- Solutions are impractical, unavailable, or interfere with the achievement objectives.
- You impinge on the rights of others and other forms of rights (e.g. protecting children from assault weapons vs. the right of children to have assault weapons).

Seeking security and resilience expertise in selecting the appropriate solution is very helpful but must be done with extreme care. Security and resilience experts are in the business of selling security, continuity, and resilience solutions. Many provide a defined range of products and solutions. Like any other business, their area of expertise will be highlighted in their advice and sales pitch. You can pick from a range of security or continuity conferences to hear presentations on "silver bullet" products and services that claim to solve various problems. You need to prioritize many risks, types of events, and scenarios within your resource allocation limitations. Managing risk is a triage activity. You need to know what questions to ask when seeking outside expertise.

There are many controls and countermeasures to choose from for all the different types of violence. Several free online compilations are listed in the bibliography of this book. Since this book focuses on the program to prevent and manage violence, rather than repeat the available literature, it refers the reader to the bibliography for additional details.

For each of the control and countermeasure strategies, develop clear policies and protocols

At an international standards development meeting, a group of "organizational resilience consultants," who predominated the group, argued that the advantage of resilience planning over risk management planning was that resilience planning assumes that there are no resource limitations while risk management considers resource limitations. They argued that the standard should reflect that planning for resilience should be based on the assumption of unlimited access to all resources (thereby increasing demand for organizational resilience consultant services). The two end-users present, who were business managers, walked out of the meeting, never to return.

for when issues need to be referred outside to law enforcement, legal authorities, or community programs. Consult legal counsel since in some jurisdictions, notification and information sharing may also be a legal requirement. Determine what the thresholds are for threat levels or level of concern to trigger contact with higher authorities in the organization as well as externally with law enforcement and emergency management personnel. These plans and threshold levels should also describe the method of communication and what information can be shared.

Another parameter to check with legal counsel is what the allowable parameters for monitoring verbal and online communications are. What are the limitations for monitoring an individual's online presence or written and verbal communications? Can computers, mobile phones, or vehicles be searched and under what conditions and in what locations? What information can be shared and with whom?

AVOIDANCE AND PREVENTION

Figure 16.5 provides a graphical depiction of a layered approach to selecting avoidance and prevention measures. Unfortunately, one of the outcomes of stress and feelings of poor self-worth, isolation, and injustice is sometimes violence. Increases in domestic, social, political, and economic tension and instability appear to serve as an escalation factor for potential violent actors. Therefore, any robust avoidance and prevention strategy should consider measures that can minimize these negative influences.

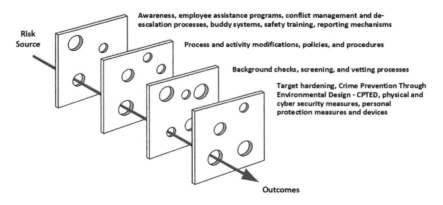

Figure 16.5   Swiss cheese model for avoidance and prevention.

Employee assistance programs, buddy systems, and reporting mechanisms provide an avenue for both troubled individuals and their potential targets to seek relief and assistance. Ironically, after every incident, some coworkers, family members, schoolmates, and neighbors give interviews to the press explaining that they saw this coming. This begs the question, "Then, why didn't you do something?" Ignoring the problem does not make it go away nor does letting people fall between the cracks, so buddy systems can help keep tabs on people of concern. Repeated awareness training on assistance and reporting programs, for both internal and external stakeholders, is an important ingredient for a successful program.

Domestic or intimate partner violence seems to have a relationship with workplace. Can a person working on your behalf find assistance in your organization or can you refer them to appropriate community assistance? Conflicts can and do occasionally spiral out of control. De-escalation training (particularly for Type II violence), mediation, and conflict resolution mechanisms can reduce stress to manageable levels to prevent violence. Consider how restraining orders are communicated and enforced while the individual is at the organization or engaged in its activities.

Consider how to develop policies and procedures and if needed, modify the process and activities to minimize the likelihood of an event and its potential consequences. Clearly defined and implemented policies, procedures, and protocols increase a sense of fairness and clarify responsibilities. Staggered schedules and flextime, cash controls, reassigning antagonists, posting pictures and access denials for persons of concern, and changing locations of operations and persons can significantly reduce risk levels while causing minimum impact on normal operations.

Termination of employment procedures should exist for normal terminations as well as those associated with violence in the organization. Too frequently, this is an activity associated with violence. Special care must be taken to protect the dignity and self-worth of the individual to avoid escalating stress levels. Procedures need to be clearly defined and equally implemented. Security measures implemented during a termination meeting should meet or exceed the potential threat level. Determine the necessary ongoing security measures needed, for example, physical and cyber access to facilities and people, notification of uninvited appearances, and key retrieval or changing. Help the individual to seek help. Never simply give a positive recommendation for an individual of concern to pass your problem to another organization.

Background checks, screening, and vetting processes should be conducted on all persons working on behalf of the organization (employees and contractors). Different jurisdictions will have different regulations related to information access and privacy, so check with legal counsel what is appropriate for your organization. Depending on the jurisdiction, background checks, screening, and vetting processes may include checks of work, employment, and education records; interviews; social media checks; reference reviews; criminal history; military records; economic and credit checks; marital and family status; physical and mental health history; driving records; weapons ownership, training, and usage habits; and substance abuse and drug use testing and history. Many professions have "fitness for duty" requirements. For your organization's activities and functions, what are the mental and physical requirements that are necessary to successfully conduct the activities and functions? When setting the requirements, consider risk factors (e.g. cash and carry, interfacing with potentially hostile and unstable clients, carrying a weapon).

Target hardening, Crime Prevention Through Environmental Design (CPTED), physical and cyber security measures, and personal protection measures and devices all significantly reduce threat levels if applied in a layered approach to deter, detect, delay, deny, defend, and respond. Document should be a complementary "D." Always document an event whether successful or not. For some issues, decoy or deflect may be a viable technique to identify a potential attack and redirect it. There is no shortage of these types of physical security measures (alarm systems, panic buttons, metal detectors, acoustic sensors, monitoring systems and surveillance equipment, landscaping and layout, guards, locks, lighting, barriers, access controls, entrance and exit controls, etc.). The key to deploying these types of measures is an understanding of their coverage and communication characteristics, response times, life cycle time frames, and their life cycle costs (particularly usage and maintenance costs). Physical security equipment has also been known to introduce serious cyber security vulnerabilities, so this should be examined. Both capital and operational expenses need to be considered when assessing security measures. Spectacular events understandably have an exaggerated sense of priority, but it is always important to understand the impacts on day-to-day operations, people working on behalf of the organization, and the trade-offs with more likely events that may have lower per event damage but significantly greater per year damage totals (e.g. workplace violence, suicides, bullying). Selection of security equipment should also consider if and how the equipment can be used for day-to-day activities. For example, can access control systems be used for employee location tracking, or can surveillance equipment also be used for process or activity monitoring? Always consider the impact on people with special needs when selecting security equipment and technologies.

PREPAREDNESS

Preparedness is an admission that something can and potentially will happen. It involves proactively planning for the management of an event to more rapidly stabilize the situation and mitigate the rate, impact, and consequences of an event. Figure 16.6 provides a graphical depiction of a layered approach to selecting preparedness measures.

Developing the emergency action plan or emergency management plan is the critical activity. It should contain all the elements illustrated in Figure 16.6. Ideally, the emergency action plan for preventing and managing violence should be aligned, if not converged, with the process failure, environmental, natural disaster, security, and safety emergency plans. There will be many overlapping issues; therefore, a comprehensive approach is more effective for sustainability.

A key part of preparedness is developing relationships and protocols for interactions with external stakeholders who will be potential actors in any emergency. This includes shared needs and requirements for information, equipment, access controls, and personnel.

Communication protocols should be clearly defined and tested. Capacity testing is essential since resources will be strained during an

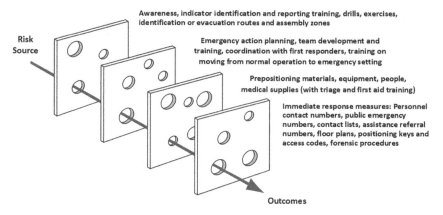

Figure 16.6 Swiss cheese model for preparedness.

159

emergency situation. The ubiquitous presence of mobile phones and communication devices is a risk that should be addressed in preparedness planning. These devices can play a vital role in communications during an event, but they can be a source of misinformation and endanger lives, particularly when victims decide that their social media presence takes precedence over safety of themselves and others. Have a defined policy and provide training, but also consider contingency planning, since, like using a mobile phone while driving, a significant portion of people simply will ignore good practice.

Awareness and training, including drills and exercises, need to be conducted regularly and repeatedly to be well absorbed by persons working on behalf of the organization, as well as to identify and assess any gaps in planning. In moments of trauma, people do not have time to read the procedures that should have been drilled into their consciousness, they must respond quickly. When developing the training and drills, assume that people will need to take responsibility for themselves and people around them and that they cannot solely depend on a chief security officer or law enforcement dealing with the incident for them. In addition to identifying and training on escape routes, there is a need for ongoing monitoring of their accessibility and compatibility for use by people with special needs. Maps and signage help, but drills using the various escape routes build the muscle memory needed for quick exiting during an actual incident. One suggestion is to have people working on behalf of the organization walk via different escape routes and entrance/exits to their workspace on an ongoing basis. People learn the various routes, as well as monitor escape routes for obstructions (any found should be immediately reported), identify potential places to seek shelter along the escape path, and can identify objects to use in self-defense along the escape path if need be. This heightens awareness and emphasizes that security is part of everyone's daily routine. At a minimum, they get some extra exercise, which benefits productivity.

Teams need to regularly and repeatedly conduct drills and exercises of their activities and functions. Drills and exercises should be documented and results carefully analyzed for opportunities for improvements. Drills should include monitoring response times and factors that impact response times, as well as human and physical capacity testing. Drills and exercises should also test the capability of team members to operate under stress.

The underlying concept of preparedness is that the more that can be prepositioned to reduce the immediate response times and to stabilize the situation, the more likely an event will not escalate into a full-blown crisis.

Start by reviewing existing plans for process failure, environmental, natural disaster, security, and safety emergencies. What needs to be added?

RESPONSE

Response will depend on the type of violence, how the event unfolds, and the time frame of events. When developing response plans, time frames for how quick the situation escalates to a crisis situation, response times, and time frames to implement plans will contribute to the outcomes. Figure 16.7 provides a graphical depiction of a layered approach to selecting response measures.

For most people, being exposed to violence is a traumatic event. This may be the first time a person has been exposed to violence directed at them, increasing the stress level. Therefore, response planning needs to consider time delays due to the body's natural response to sudden extreme stress and the uncertainties (physical and mental) of the opening moments of an event. Rapidly accelerated heartbeat and blood pressure rates will distort human senses (sight, sound, and motor skills). Stress relief exercise training (power breathing, touching objects, taking a knee, etc.) can help anchor a person more quickly so that their senses return to a functional level. Regular and repeated exercises help build muscle memory that may help control stress levels and shorten response times but this is highly dependent on an individual during a real event. Stress reduction techniques can also contribute to increased productivity in day-to-day

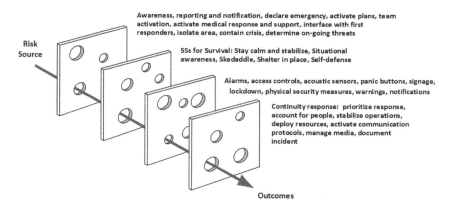

Figure 16.7 Swiss cheese model for response.

activities. Devise an approach that can address day-to-day stress (a preventative measure) and that will help keep people cool headed during a crisis. Years ago, while giving security management lectures to government workers in China, regular breaks were included for mandated tai chi exercises. There was a discernable uptick in energy and attention in the audience after each break.

Violent events may unfold rapidly and bring profound changes to one's surroundings. Situational awareness is therefore paramount to survival and safety. During the opening round of gunfire, it is very difficult for people to ascertain the origin or amount of shots fired, or even to determine if it is gunfire, a car backfire, or fireworks. Do you try to escape not knowing if you will run into the gunman or become snared in a trap? After calming and stabilizing your senses, the next step is taking stock to determine your course of action. Situational awareness considers the environment around you and what your options are. Situational awareness also considers how to safely alert others to the developing crisis; therefore, preplanned alerting and communication mechanisms (alarms, panic buttons, text messages, etc.) should be developed and training on the mechanisms should be conducted as a proactive measure.

Many training programs exist describing personal response options (e.g. the US Department of Security's "Run, Hide, Fight" program). The two key elements just described (stabilizing and situational awareness) are essential for determining, that given the current situation, which path is the best to follow and in what order and time frame. The response will depend on the nature of the event and how it is unfolding. Keep this in mind when determining what equipment and technologies to use to augment escaping, hiding, or confronting an assailant. Equipment and technologies may provide benefits in only limited scenarios, may complicate response in a different scenario, or may even be leveraged by an aware assailant familiar with the defenses.

Incorporating stabilizing and situational awareness into the "Run, Hide, Fight" approach, consider the "5Ss for Survival" (© M Siegel Associates LLC):

- Stay calm and stabilize: Allow your body and your senses to stabilize.
- Situational awareness: Gauge your surrounds and determine a course of action.
- Skedaddle: Is escape or evacuation a viable option? Do you know if you are running away from or into trouble? Before an incident,

familiarize yourself with egress procedures and escape routes. Maintain clear paths of exit.

- Shelter-in-place: Is hiding or barricading yourself in a safe place an option? Is lockdown possible? Before an incident, familiarize yourself with shelter-in-place locations when practicing egress procedures and escape routes to determine safe zones along the path of escape.
- Self-defense: Do you and those with you have a better chance of survival by confronting an assailant? When, where, and how do you have a chance of mounting a successful self-defense approach? When familiarizing with egress procedures and escape routes familiarize yourself with common elements in the surroundings that you can use to confront or distract an assailant. For example, fire extinguishers are both blinding agents and clubs. Throwing objects can distract or injure an assailant. Making a move when a gunman is reloading can give you precious seconds to make a difference.

When training people how to skedaddle, make sure they are informed how to interface and present themselves to first responders (e.g. exit with hands extended and exposed). Remember that law enforcement's top concern when entering a violent and often confusing situation is to neutralize the assailant to stop further damage.

Determine what the appropriate assembly areas for different types of incidents are and associated training needs. Keep in mind that panic frequently accompanies violent acts, and people might seek what they perceive as a safer location than designated assembly areas. Have a communication protocol, with contact information in both directions, to facilitate locating and reunifying people.

When developing a response plan, determine and assign roles for what triggers what response mechanisms and who has the authority to activate plans and

During a full-scale exercise testing a scenario of a terrorist attack on a school coupled with a follow-up attack on the local hospital, it was discovered that the phone system at the school and the hospital were overwhelmed by parents searching for their children. Not only did this lead to confusion, it restricted the hospital's ability to contact additional medical staff to manage the sudden large influx of victims. School, hospital, and community notification systems were reviewed and improved to avoid a repeat of these capacity limitations and enhance communications.

mobilize resources. Who and how is an emergency declared and how are people notified of the crisis? Teams, first responder notification, emergency response equipment and procedures, communication protocols, containment and isolation processes, medical response, and the continuity plan will all need to be activated.

Similar to other disruptive events that result from intentional, unintentional, and natural causes, normal activities and services will be disrupted. Develop or revisit your business continuity plan to include potential consequences of an act of violent of various types. Planning should consider minimizing degradation of activities and impact on individuals, managing the extent of degradation of activities and services, prioritizing critical activities needed to be reinstated to assure survival of the organization, and identifying time frame and resources needed for recovery.

RECOVERY

Post-incident recovery and assessment is an essential component of any program to prevent and manage violence. A recovery plan is more effective when combined with continuity plans. Investigation and assessment of the incident needs to go beyond just documenting and collecting forensic evidence of the event but also include gathering data to analyze root causes to determine corrective and preventive measure to prevent a recurrence. Figure 16.8 provides a graphical depiction of a layered approach to selecting recovery measures.

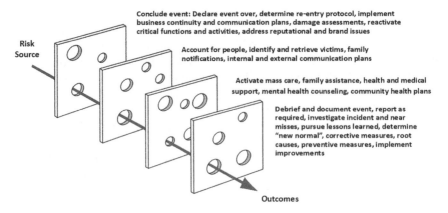

Figure 16.8 Swiss cheese model for recovery.

Immediate victims as well as members of the larger communities involved will likely manifest signs of short- and/or long-term trauma which may manifest themselves as guilt feelings, changes in interpersonal relationships, fear of being in the organization, lost productivity, or criticism or accusations about other persons touched by the event. There seems to be a need for people to understand why to bring an event to closure. Unfortunately, the answer might not be forthcoming. Care, counseling, and assistance programs should be available through the organization and in the community.

Investigations should be about identifying facts and evidence about what, how, and why something happened. Avoid scapegoating and looking for someone to blame. Having witnessed wars, terror attacks, and other violent acts, one thing is certain, there are few obvious heroes and most people freeze or are disoriented before they can react effectively. Only the dead, or someone never confronted by deathly violence, believe that they could storm into a building barehanded to confront a violent, armed assailant set on causing the death of others.

Recovery plans should address how to declare the immediate event over, assess the damage and any ongoing threats or potential copycat events, account for all individuals, reinstate critical functions, and activate continuity and recovery activities. Communication protocols should address family reunifications, notification of injuries and death along with resources the organization can direct to help victims, reporting requirements, and dealing with the community and media.

Investigation procedures should address legal, regulatory, and liability issues and collecting forensic evidence, as well as considering operational issues. Investigations and reporting should cover what, how, and why events took place. Investigation procedures should be defined, consistent, and documented. The simplest root-cause analysis method is to answer a question with a question by asking "why" five times in sequence.

After a violent event, there is no "returning to normal." Events should be learning experiences, and a "new normal" should be determined using lessons learned. While many factors leading to an event might be clear in hindsight, ask why they were not anticipated and could something different have been done. Be careful using hindsight; it is 20/20. "How did we not notice the student was socially awkward!?" Maybe because being socially awkward is a rite of passage of many teenagers. Is there really something that could have identified the needle in the haystack without causing other effects? The greater the magnitude of an event, the more overly critical people will be while the shock of the event is still fresh in their minds. Do both a hot debrief immediately after the event, followed by a cold debrief after emotions and stress have cooled. Does the analysis change? Do you see different issues than were "obvious" in the heat of moment? Was there a gap between signs of danger and action to mitigate danger, if so how can this be improved?

The threat assessment team, supplemented with necessary external expertise (first responders), and top management representatives should review the entire program for prevention and managing violence to iden-tify opportunities for improve. After the event, the risk environment has changed so that it is time to revisit the risk assessment procedures and outcomes. Avoid snap equipment purchases before conducting a root cause analysis since you might be making procurements that are not con-sistent with the real risk but rather the perceived risk after an event.

Part of the recovery process is recognizing the problem of violence in organizations may change, but it will never disappear. Therefore, ongoing vigilance and an attitude of continual improvement drive actions going forward.

EXAMPLE OF STANDARD OPERATING PROCEDURE

Standard operating procedures provide a blueprint for measures to be taken to consistently achieve desired outcomes. Integrating the manage-ment of risk into standard operating procedures helps build an awareness of what risks are associated with the procedure and the stakeholders who can impact or be impacted by the procedure. Procedures should specify the following:

1. The purpose of the procedure
2. The scope of the procedure
3. Assets, activities, and functions targeted by the procedure and their criticality to objectives
4. Risks associated with and addressed by the procedure
5. Internal and external stakeholders who are impacted by the procedure
6. Internal and external stakeholders who can impact the procedure and outcomes

7. Internal and external interdependencies, dependencies, and interactions
8. Objectives of the procedure and measures of success
9. Implementation steps and the frequency with which the procedure is carried out
10. Roles, responsibilities, and authorities including appropriate lead
11. Resource requirements (including linkages to other processes)
12. Communication requirements, protocols, and procedures
13. Resource, competency, and training requirements
14. Information flow and documentation processes
15. Key performance indicators
16. Review and revision procedure and time frames

It is good practice to identify the primary person responsible for the procedure including responsibility for reviewing, amending, and updating the procedure. The process of accessing, reviewing, amending, updating, and distributing procedures should be controlled.

17

Active Shooter—Things You Need to Know (Example of Active Shooter Flyer)

Who is an active shooter?

An individual actively engaged in killing or attempting to kill people.

Typically, there is no pattern or method to their selection of victims.

Active shooter situations are unpredictable and evolve quickly.

Active shooter situations are often over within 10–15 minutes—frequently before law enforcement arrives.

The likelihood of being in an active shooter event is very low, but you need to be prepared both mentally and physically to deal with an active shooter situation.

Are Active Shooter Events Impulsive Acts? Are There Signs to Look For?

Although *there is no "profile" of an active shooter* they are rarely impulsive acts.

"See Something, Say Something"—there are often warning signs, too often discovered in 20-20 hindsight, so report behaviors that may seem to be predictors of violence.

Denial or an "it can't happen here" attitude does not work—better to seek and report suspicious behavior and be wrong than later discover that there were warning signs dismissed because you were afraid to be wrong. Family and friends' common post-incident questions include the following: How did I not see this coming? Why did I not take him (96% of assailants are men) seriously?

Some *common indicators and triggers* include the following: life changing events (deaths, divorce, job loss, financial problems); self-righteousness (protecting a value system that makes violence acceptable, blaming others, resentment); fascination with violence (fixation on violent incidents, games, or weapons); "otherness" (designating people as outsiders, sense of persecution); mental illness (depression, paranoia, excessive emotional responses); bullying, humiliation, alienation, and rejection; and sudden changes in behavior patterns. Designate individuals within your organization as a *"threat assessment team"* who can address concerns and create both open and anonymous mechanisms for reporting suspicious behaviors.

Security Awareness—How Do I Get Started?

Individuals

Stay calm and stabilize: The first thing you will notice when you are involved in a stressful or violent act is that your body automatically responds with elevated heartbeat and blood pressure, resulting in decreased cognitive capacity and coordination. Your survival depends on your senses and ability to think. *Practice "tactical 4 × 4 breathing" or "take a knee" techniques* to calm yourself. Spending a few seconds (3–5 breaths) on calming techniques will heighten your awareness and ability to function. Hopefully, you will never need these techniques for a violent event, but it will make you a better athlete and a calmer person. Assess the situation and environment before deciding next steps.

Situational awareness: Gage your surroundings and determine a course of action. Stay alert and try to determine where the threat is coming from. If you think an attacker is in a certain area, do not make your escape in that direction and warn others of the assailant's location if possible.

- Skedaddle: Know your environment. *Escape when possible*, so have a plan. Familiariz[e] yourself with escape routes in your surrounding area—know multiple exit routes. G[et] some exercise—walk in and out of buildings via different routes to familiarize yourse[lf] with routes and observe if there are any obstructions or areas to hide.
- Shelter-in-place: If escape is not an option, *find a safe place to hide*. Stay out of sight and avoi[d] a clear path for bullets. Keep your options open—position yourself for a potential escap[e] or to overwhelm an attacker. Lock and block the door. Be quiet—both you and your phon[e.] Continue your calming techniques to heighten your awareness and ability to function. Do n[ot] come out of hiding if you are safe and until you can verify the identity of a potential rescue[r.]
- Self-defense: If escaping and hiding are not options, *you may need to fight or incapacita[te] the assailant.* Team action works better to overwhelm an assailant but you may need to a[ct] alone. Commit to your action and target the assailant where it really hurts (eyes, hea[d,] throat, groin). Look around you and plan ahead—what can be weaponized? Noise di[s]tracts, close quarters reduces the attacker's freedom of motion, scissors and pens are sta[b]bing devices, dry chemical fire extinguishers are both a blinding agent and a blunt for[ce] object. What would James Bond use?
- *When first responders arrive*, let them do their job. Follow their instructions, it is not about yo[u,] it is now about securing the area. Keep your hands visible, fingers spread, and in the ope[n.] Share information about the assailant and your level of certainty about that information[.]
- For all the above options, *run "what if" scenarios in your head*—if the zombies come [in] through the front door where do you go? What if they come in from the other direction[?] What if they are already among you? How do you stay out of the reach of the killin[g] machine? What is close at hand to use as a barricade or to fight with? Compassion seldo[m] works once the killing starts.

Organizations

- Have a plan—although active shooter events are less likely than most security threat[s,] fire or natural disasters, they need to be part of your risk management and emergen[cy] management plans.
- "Plans are nothing; planning is everything"—Dwight D. Eisenhower. Know yo[ur] objectives and goals. Learn to anticipate. Share the thought process and help peop[le] understand why they are doing things so that they can improvise when needed. Practi[ce] your plans, but question "what if" the event unfolds differently from the plan.
- Provide open and anonymous mechanisms for people to express their concerns witho[ut] fear or embarrassment.
- Designate multiple evacuation routes, safe areas, and assembly points. Determine how [to] provide warnings to people when an emergency occurs. Do not forget people with speci[al] needs. Drill everyone in your organization—remember leaders lead by example, dril[ls] need to include everyone.
- The first time you meet your first responders should not be when they are respondin[g.] Have contact information for the police, fire fighters, and local area hospitals han[dy] (including speed dial—you will probably be distracted if an event occurs). Determi[ne] their response times. Assign people the responsibility to contact help. Invite law enforc[e]ment and other first responders to participate in your drills.
- Help first responders do their job. Have floor plans of your facility available for respon[d]ers and critical personnel. Keys and security pass codes need to be made accessible to fir[st] responders. Conduct a walk-through with first responders before an event occurs.
- Maintain updated contact information. Have staff roster and emergency contact inform[a]tion accessible before, during, and after an event. Assign people to make sure they c[an] access this information during a crisis.
- First responders need to first neutralize the threat. Have first aid and triage kits availab[le] for easy access and have people trained on how to treat trauma until help arrives.

Section IV

Closure

18

Closing Thoughts

Violence has plagued humans from the beginning of time and will likely be with us until the end of time. Researchers will continue to study why some people exposed to the same stimulus and environment act out violently while others do not. From a risk management perspective, violence in organizations should always be considered an uncertainty in achieving objectives. Duty of care mandates that violence is a risk that must be assessed and treated.

Violence is a risk that can happen to anyone, anywhere, with or without prior warning. It is not a risk that can be managed by a single individual or division in an organization. It is a risk that can impact or be impacted by everyone providing or receiving services from an organization's activities. Therefore, to be successful, programs to prevent and manage violence need to be seamlessly integrated into the organization's core business and risk management program. It is not a standalone activity.

Equipment and technologies can help prevent and manage violence, but awareness programs empowering people to manage the risks they impact or are impacted by are essential elements of any program. By building a sense of responsibility to manage risks in all day-to-day activities coupled with a "we're in this all together" attitude, organizations can better manage violence-related uncertainties. Inclusion builds a sense of ownership.

Organizations need to move from an ad hoc and reactionary approach to a formal, proactive approach based on good risk and business management practice. Unfortunately, since violence has the potential to disrupt any type or size of organization, it must be addressed as part of managing any type of risk facing a business, school, or house of worship.

The starting point is building in, rather than adding on, a system of management to prevent and manage violence into the organization's overall system of management. This book provides the ingredients to the recipe for doing this. When deciding the path forward for your organization, keep in mind the outcome you are looking for is a cultural change for security and risk awareness in the organization. Cultural change is successful when it is paced to the capacity of people working on behalf of the organization to absorb the changes. Change management requires an implementation plan, management commitment, and benchmarks of success along the path.

Violence touches us all and rightfully is a very emotional and litigious subject to address. Decision making is complicated by the desire to protect human life or make the problem go away at any cost. The reality is that there are not unlimited resources available to try to eliminate all risks related to violence. Preventing and managing violence requires tough decisions about how to best allocate resources to protect people and achieve the organization's objectives. By focusing risk management on the uncertainty in achievement of objectives, rather than simply looking at the threats of singular events, users of this book can make decisions based on facts and information (rather than emotions) how to most effectively protect its most precious asset—people.

This book provides tools using the basic principles of risk management to support decision making. Every organization must tailor an approach to fit its needs and culture. You cannot make the problem disappear, nor can you deny the problem, nor can you predict the future. But you can take control and establish a program to minimize the likelihood and consequences of violence in your organization.

19

Bibliography of Additional Materials

Below is a partial list of websites providing a plethora of free information on preventing and managing violence in organizations. Go to the website and enter keywords in the search box (workplace violence, active shooter, emergency management plan, domestic violence, etc.) to get a list of all materials available on the topic:

Centers for Disease Control and Prevention, Violence Prevention: www.cdc.gov/violenceprevention/index.html

Committee of Sponsoring Organizations of the Treadway Commission (COSO), *COSO Enterprise Risk Management – Integrated Framework*, 2017: www.coso.org/Pages/erm-integratedframework.aspx

International Labour Organization, Prevention of Violence at Work: www.ilo.org/safework/areasofwork/workplace-health-promotion-and-well-being/WCMS_108511/lang--en/index.htm

International Organization for Standardization, ISO31000:2018 Risk Management – Guidance standard, 2018: www.iso.org/iso-31000-risk-management.html

National Center for Campus Public Safety: www.nccpsafety.org/

National Crime Prevention Council, Be Safe and Sound in School: www.ncpc.org/programs/be-safe-and-sound-in-school/

National Domestic Violence Hotline: www.thehotline.org/

National PTA, School Safety: www.pta.org/home/family-resources/safety/School-Safety

National Safety Council: www.nsc.org/work-safety/safety-topics/workplace-violence

Safe Work Australia, Workplace Violence: www.safeworkaustralia.gov.au/workplace-violence

United Kingdom Health and Safety Executive, Work-related Violence: www.hse.gov.uk/violence/index.htm

United States Department of Health and Human Services, Emergency Operations Plans: www.phe.gov/preparedness/planning/pages/eops.aspx

United States Department of Homeland Security, Active Shooter Preparedness: www.dhs.gov/active-shooter-preparedness

United States Department of Homeland Security, Center for Faith-Based & Neighborhood Partnerships: www.fema.gov/faith

United States Department of Justice, Office of Violence against Women: www.justice.gov/ovw

United States Department of Labor, Occupational Safety and Health Administration, Evacuation and Shelter-in-Place: www.osha.gov/SLTC/emergencypreparedness/gettingstarted_evacuation.html

United States Department of Labor, Occupational Safety and Health Administration, Workplace Violence: www.osha.gov/SLTC/workplaceviolence/

United States Department of Labor, Occupational Safety and Health Administration, Workplace Violence Prevention Programs: www.osha.gov/SLTC/workplaceviolence/evaluation.html

United States Department of Labor, Workplace Violence Program: www.dol.gov/oasam/hrc/policies/dol-workplace-violence-program.htm

United States Federal Bureau of Investigations, Office of Partner Engagement, Active Shooter Resources: www.fbi.gov/about/partnerships/office-of-partner-engagement/active-shooter-resources

United States Federal Bureau of Investigations, Uniform Crime Reporting (UCR) Program: https://ucr.fbi.gov/

United States Secret Service, National Threat Assessment Center: www.secretservice.gov/protection/ntac/

INDEX